Exceptional Pregnancies:

A Survival Guide to Parents Expecting Triplets or More

Cover Photo: The Storey family, Dunwoody, Georgia
(Photo by Wendy Hilsinger, Rochester, New York)

Exceptional Pregnancies

A Survival Guide to Parents Expecting Triplets or More

Kathleen S. Birch
and
Janet L. Bleyl

ISBN 0-9676161-0-7

For information address:

The Triplet Connection
P.O. Box 99571
Stockton, CA 95209

Phone (209) 474-0885 • Fax (209) 474-2233

E-Mail address: tc@tripletconnection.org
Internet address: http://www.tripletconnection.org

FIRST EDITION

Designed by CM, Elm Street Press

Foreword

Forty years ago, while a medical resident, I participated in the delivery of a triplet pregnancy – which at the time was a rare event. There were 28 individuals in the delivery room, including one priest who was in the far corner of the delivery room praying. Currently, a triplet pregnancy is not such a momentous event for an institution or community; however, it still remains an exciting and emotional event for both the patient and the physician.

Assisted reproductive technologies (ART) have accounted for the rising rate of twins and higher-order multiple gestation over the past 20 years. The birth rate for triplet and other higher-order multifetal gestation has increased from 37 per 100,000 live births in 1980 to 127.5 per 100,000 live births in 1995. The maternal risks associated with higher-order multiples relate to pre-eclampsia, gestational diabetes mellitus, preterm labor, preterm premature rupture of membranes, risks associated with cesarean delivery, acute fatty liver and cardiomyopathy. Not to be overlooked are the post partum complications such as hemorrhage, extreme stress and depression, psychosocial adjustments related to parenting, marital strain, divorce, and financial hardship. Fetal risks with higher-order multiples relate to intrauterine growth restriction, fetal anomalies and premature delivery.

The book *Exceptional Pregnancies: A Survival Guide to Parents Expecting Triplets or More* is a labor of love. Kathleen S. Birch and Janet L. Bleyl have garnered together resources that will allow parents of higher-order multiples to prepare for all eventualities. The authors' personal experiences and attestations of other parents of higher-order multiples are both educational for prospective parents of multi-fetal gestations and illuminating reading for physicians caring for prospective parents of multi-fetal gestations.

This is an age of knowledge and information. The Internet provides patients a ready source of information to guide them through the excitement, frustrations, fear and elation of a multiple fetal pregnancy. Our "consumers" of health care have become "prosumers," active participants in their care. Pregnancy outcome can most effectively be improved by integrating the skills and knowledge of the physicians as well as concerns and questions of well-informed patients.

It is obvious that the authors have tried to emphasize that where there is care and caring of patients, everyone benefits. Throughout the chapters there is an intermingling of basic and sophisticated information necessary to address the complex issues of higher-order multiple pregnancy. Given the emotional and ethically charged nature of such pregnancies, the authors have attempted to bring forth a collection of balanced views addressing many risk/benefit ratios of each of the potential conundrums met by parents and physicians. The book is not a set of rigid and obstructive regulations between physician and patient, but it is a bridge which allows open communication between the physician and the patient. In particular physicians should read the quotations from patients who have "walked the walk and talked the talk." The quotations are clear sources of edification and reflection.

It has been said that we do not know the cause or causes of preterm labor, how to diagnose it or how to treat it; however, the presentation of information in the book on this subject does give many options that answer the above three areas. Patients and physicians will do well to maintain a balanced view rather than adopting the concept of therapeutic nihilism when faced with the greatest challenge of multiple fetal pregnancy. We should set the sails to take advantage of the winds as well as steer the course that will allow the patient to be in optimal medical and emotional care.

We must understand that fertility drugs as well as other reproductive technologies have been welcomed by thousands of parents and that despite the judicious use of ovulatory agents and limiting the number of transferred embryos from in-vitro fertilization treatment, higher-order multiple gestations persist. We should not place our patients in difficult ethical dilemmas nor should we place our patients in harm's way. The book presents a balanced overview of the challenges of multiple fetal reduction.

The physicians who are quoted in this book are recognized for their training and experience. They are dedicated and skilled physicians, committed to the ensurance that every pregnant patient receives the best care possible. Their quotations clearly emphasize their experiences, which have not always been positive; but at least they try to become role models in the art of caring and are dedicated physicians willing to accept the physical and emotional highs and lows associated with preparing a mother and father of multiple fetal pregnancy.

The authors should be congratulated for pulling together a collection of real life experiences that can serve as a beacon for parents of multi-fetal pregnancy so that a condition that was once described as hopeless can now be transformed into the joy of delivering healthy, normal babies.

"Life is short, art is long, occasion fleeting, attempt perilous, and judgement difficult."

–Hippocrates

Robert C. Cefalo MD, PhD
Clinical Professor, Obstetrics & Gynecology
University of North Carolina School of Medicine
Chapel Hill, North Carolina

Madeleine, Gray and Hannah Birch, Cody, Wyoming

To every expectant parent of multiples.
May you know the joy of parenting on a grand scale!
To my husband, Jeff; my wonderful children, Jeffrey,
Tom, Rebecca, Justin, Jared, Shannon, Joseph, Jacob,
Jonathan, and Whitney; and my beautiful grandchil-
dren, Jessica, Benjamin, Bradley, Jordan, Shelby,
Aleissa, Stephan, Misaki and Ariah.

— *Janet Bleyl*

To my children – Madeleine, Hannah and Gray –
who have given me the joys of parenting times three.
And to my husband, Warren, who supported me
during this challenging endeavor.

— *Kathleen Birch*

ABOUT THE AUTHORS

Kathleen S. Birch, M.A., mother of fraternal
triplets, former cancer researcher, and tireless
champion of "our common cause"
resides in Cody, Wyoming, with her husband,
Dr. Warren Birch, and their children, Madeleine,
Hannah and Gray.
This publication has become a reality as a
result of her dedication and committed work.

Janet L. Bleyl, founder and president
of The Triplet Connection, is a mother of
ten children, including identical triplets Joseph,
Jacob and Jonathan born December 16, 1982.
Married to Jeffrey A. Bleyl since 1967, her family
lives in Stockton, California, where she works
full-time trying to help parents of multiples
know the joy and the miracle of a healthy birth.
Every member of her family has been involved
in The Triplet Connection, the national
"Network of Caring and Sharing for Multiple
Birth Families," which she founded.

OUR THANKS

This publication would never have been completed without the help and support of numerous individuals. Our heartfelt thanks first, to our wonderful and supportive husbands, who have taken care of children, fixed dinners, shuttled and entertained, read and re-read manuscripts, massaged shoulders, and slept alone for many, many nights. Thanks to our patient and long-suffering children. All have done without their moms on numerous occasions, have played quietly or "gotten by" while we worked, have been content with pizza and Cheerios, and "moved over" when we got together in one another's homes to work.

Thanks to each member of the Scientific Advisory Board of The Triplet Connection for their input and comments, their support and advice, their willingness to answer questions and provide information at inopportune times. Special thanks to each for their dedication to all multiple birth families as they continue to meet together in support of our efforts.

Thanks to dedicated, hard-working secretaries Georgia Stewart and Juliene Miller, who've held down the fort for days and weeks on end, and who have offered many valuable suggestions and support.

Thanks to Carol Marceau, who worked diligently to publish our first book, and who helped put ideas into a professional, fun format. Thanks to Liberty Press, which worked and re-worked our ideas into the book you now hold.

Thanks to every parent of multiples who has taken the time and effort to complete and return a detailed medical questionnaire, who has reached out in caring and sharing for others who enter the world of multiple birth, and who has shared his/her experiences – both good and bad – for the benefit of those who follow.

Thanks to doctors who give great service, expertise, and care to moms and dads and children, and who continue to explore new and better ways to enhance improved outcomes.

Thanks to modern science and technology for computers and faxes and airplanes and telephones – the tools that have made our organization blossom and our efforts successful.

Most of all, we thank the Lord for the blessings of life, family, and friends.

Kathleen and Janet

The Gibbons children, Irvine, California

Table of Contents

The Farmer family, Lynwood, Washington

What You Need to Know About Us and This Book

About The Triplet Connection

A Bit of Background

by Janet Bleyl

As parents of triplets, quadruplets and quintuplets, you are *not* alone in the world! There *is* valuable information available (and much more coming all the time) to help you through your pregnancies, or to help you adjust to and cope with triplets or more in your lives. There are so many others to network with who, having gone through similar experiences, would love to be of help!

I will never forget my own triplet pregnancy. My physician was honestly not sure how to handle the pregnancy. An experienced and competent obstetrician, he did his homework, calling every high-risk medical facility around. For every piece of advice he received, he got two other contrasting opinions. Together, he and I decided to play it by ear. Though my babies were actually born 10 1/2 weeks prematurely, we fortunately had decided to make sure I was in a Level III Neonatal Intensive Care Unit hospital for the birth of my triplets; otherwise, I feel sure my three healthy, identical boys would not be with us today.

There was *nobody* to talk with – nobody who understood, anyway. There was *nothing* to read that was worth reading regarding triplet pregnancies, either for me or my physician. Though I had previously given birth to six children, I felt absolutely panic-stricken at the prospect of caring for three tiny babies all at the same time. I didn't have the foggiest idea of how to prepare for the task. My instincts told me that I would find a way to care for them if only I could bring them to a healthy birth, but there were so many things that I had to learn through experience that I would rather have *read* about.

During pregnancy, I thought ahead to my triplets' growing up. I wondered how others made out, how they coped with raising triplets or growing up triplets themselves. I wondered if they felt resentful of the "mistakes" their parents made, and supposed that surely adult triplets could be our best teachers!

I felt that parents of adult and older triplets could be invaluable sources of information, but I didn't know where in the world to find others. In all my life I had never met another triplet person, and I didn't know anyone else who knew of any, either. My local Mothers of Twins group was here, but there were no local mothers of triplets on their roster.

After an incredible pregnancy (I've had one doctor correct me on the term "incredible," remarking that the pregnancy was perhaps unusual, but certainly not incredible. Of course, this doctor has never yet managed a triplet pregnancy.)... as I was saying... After an INCREDIBLE pregnancy, I found myself the mother of three of the tiniest, sickest, little-old-men-looking babies. I had not been ready for the pregnancy, with all the extreme discomforts and problems. I was scared to death of the c-section itself (brave though I may seem, I'm really a coward at heart). I was totally shocked at the condition of my babies when they were born.

I expected, after enduring all I had before the babies' birth, to be able to go on with my life with the greatest of ease. What I found, instead, was a shock to me. The pregnancy had been physically and emotionally exhausting. The c-section was major surgery. The babies were given a 50-50 chance for survival, and I was too sick to see them for two days. When I finally did see them, they scared me to death! Though I had breastfed all my previous babies because I felt it was best for them, I had no intention of even attempting to breastfeed triplets (I seemed to be ill equipped for the job!). When I looked at those critically ill little sweethearts, though, I decided *for sure* they would have my milk as soon as they were able to take nourishment. Of course, my doctors, nurses, family and best friends all assured me that I would never successfully nurse them.

So, sick and hurting and scared, I hooked myself up to an electric breastpump. I have to say, life did not seem wonderful and happy at that point in time. I didn't even feel like those three little babies who were 60 miles away in a hospital were mine; instead, I felt like I was watching three tiny strangers struggling for their lives, but never feeling like they were really *my* babies! (I've come to understand since then that it is *normal* for parents of critically ill newborns to delay bonding— a barrier against the possible pain of their loss. It is, nevertheless, up-

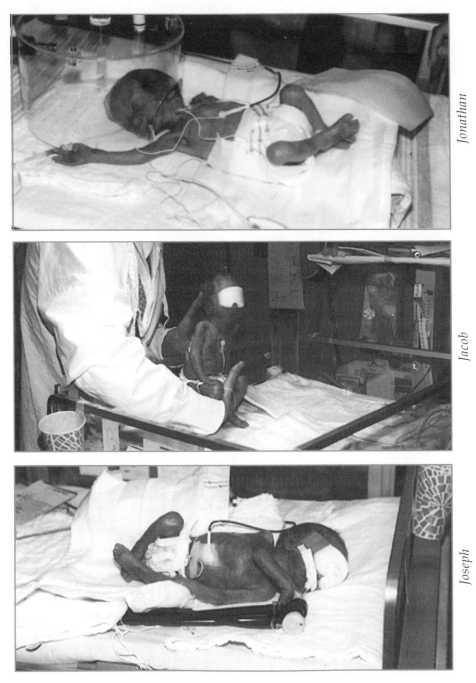

Jonathan

Jacob

Joseph

Our triplets at about three weeks.

Jonathan, Joseph and Jacob at 9 years.
I believe in miracles!

setting and difficult to experience that vacuum of feeling for babies you've waited so long to love.) And I got *no* cuddly, satisfying feeling whatever when I stroked that breast pump (it just about sucks your breasts off!).

That's how I began life as a mother of triplets—with a broken body, a broken heart, and feeling as though there was no one on God's green earth who could understand or advise me.

I want you to know right now that it all got better! We traveled back and forth nightly for nine weeks, carrying breast milk on ice, and hoping to see improvement in our sweet sons. They fluctuated between doing well and having serious setbacks almost daily. The day we finally brought them home seemed a miracle, a joy we could hardly comprehend. How unprepared we were, though, for the never-ending marathon of meeting the needs of our tiny, still-sick infants who each required feedings every two hours (each feeding taking more than an hour to accomplish) around the clock.

In time, our three sons grew and developed. Though it was a challenge, it became a joyous experience. That maternal instinct did arrive, and even now I can't get enough of those beautiful children whom I love more than life itself. I cannot express how very fortunate and blessed I feel.

Realizing what a void of medical information there was for my doctor to draw from during my pregnancy, I felt sure that as soon as my babies were born my case would be thoroughly studied and compared with other such pregnancies. Not so. My medical journey went no further than the file cabinet, and there was no interest anywhere in learning from what I had just endured. When I talked with my doctor about the possibility of beginning research in the area of larger multiple pregnancies, he assured me that it could not be done. "With triplets occurring only once in 10,000 cases, it would be impossible." You know, I had learned by experience that some of the decisions made concerning the management of my pregnancy hadn't turned out to be the best-all-round for me or my babies. My doctor had learned some valuable lessons too, but as he explained to me, he would never likely manage another triplet pregnancy in his career.

In telling me that it was impossible to conduct effective research on such pregnancies, my doctor was telling me the wrong thing. An obstinate beast by nature, if ever anyone *really* wants to see me do a thing, his best advice may be to tell me I *can't* do it, or it can't be done! It was as good as done! When I contemplated how many women would endure the same experience I had just been through without benefitting one bit from the mistakes and successes of my own experience, and how many women had already traveled that road previously without benefitting others, I decided that something surely must be done; if no one else was doing it, I would!

With this in mind, I began searching for other triplet parents. I found one, living about 15 miles away with three darling little girls. I worked with her to unearth every triplet we could find, and on August 16, 1983, had the first meeting of the then-unnamed Triplet Connection. We had ten sets of triplets and their families together that day, as well as an expectant mother of triplets, and I can't tell you how wonderful it was to share ideas, fun and experiences. That week I began a quarterly newsletter which has now reached thousands of families of triplets, quadruplets, and more.

Slowly, we began to network families, physicians, medical records and experiences together. The Triplet Connection has now been involved with helping thousands of individuals through their pregnancies, helping them to prepare both before and afterwards for the transition of three or more little miracles into their lives. We've connected families all over the U.S. and abroad, sharing happiness and sadness, good experiences and bad. We've received the interest and support of many competent and caring medical professionals who share with us the desire to help expectant mothers carry their babies to a healthy outcome, and we have received back more than 10,000 detailed medical questionnaires, giving us a bird's eye view of what *is* and what *is not* effective in carrying these high-risk infants safely into the world. We maintain a roster of over 19,000 families, and our quarterly newsletter was last sent to 8,000 locations. Approximately 2,000 *expectant* parents will receive our packet of information this year. We also have a yearly convention where an average of more than 100 families of higher-order multiples meet together to revel in the joy and miracle of our wonderful children.

At our meetings and through our newsletters we have been able to interview adult triplets who have told us what is great and what is not about having grown up with their multiple siblings. Parents and grandparents have shared and given us warnings about what has and has not been effective for them. Expectant moms are learning that there are effective ways to cope with their pregnancies and to avoid premature birth; they're learning that they can successfully breastfeed triplets or quadruplets if they so desire, and that there are many ways to ease the burden of the care and keeping of their babies. Ten-year-olds who don't particularly like being triplets at present are finding that they are normal (and their parents are being reassured of that fact, too). And, for those unfortunate families who lose through prematurity or illness one or more of their precious infants or who face long-term problems related to their birth, we have wonderful, compassionate networking opportunities.

And that is what the Triplet Connection is all about. It is an opportunity for all of us, in whatever way we are involved with larger multiples, to *share*. We don't have all the answers. Better pregnancy management definitely is on the horizon, and our combined experiences are doing a lot to help make larger multiple births less hazardous. For right now, our aim is to provide resources to those who can benefit by them, giving hope and encouragement to those who need it.

We hope that you might find The Triplet Connection to be a source of help and encouragement, and we look forward to hearing more from you! More than anything, we want you to know that we're here as a resource for you, and that we **care**.

Triplet Connection Scientific Advisory Board

Amy Alvarez, M.D., Medical Director, Anesthesiologist, Our Lady of Victory Surgery Center, Orchard Park, NY, Triplet Mother

Kathleen S. Birch M.A., Cancer Researcher, Writer, Cody, WY, Triplet Mother

Tuvia Blechman, M.D., Director, Level III+ Newborn Intensive Care Unit, Howard County General Hospital; Chairman, Department of Pediatrics, Maryland

Janet L. Bleyl, President and Founder, The Triplet Connection, Stockton, CA, Triplet Mother

Joseph V. Collea, M.D., Professor, Division Maternal Fetal Medicine, Georgetown Medical Center, Washington, D.C.

Michael S. Collins, M.D., Clinical Instructor OBGYN, Oregon Health Science University: Dept. Chairman OBGYN, Good Samaritan Hospital, Portland, OR, Triplet Father.

Nancy J. Eaton, R.N., BSN, Beth Israel Deaconess Medical Center, Boston, MA

John P. Elliott, M.D., Associate Director, Maternal Fetal Medicine, Good Samaritan Regional Medical Center, Phoenix, AZ

Allen DeVaney Elster, M.D., Department of Radiology, Bowman Gray School of Medicine Wake Forest University, Winston-Salem, NC, Triplet Father

Pamela Gill, R.N., MSN, Coordinator of the Preterm Birth Prevention Program at Children's Hospital of San Francisco; Assistant Clinical Professor, Dept. of Family Health Care, Nursing,University of California, San Francisco, CA, Twin Mother

Boyd W. Goetzman, M.D., Professor of Pediatrics, Division of Neonatology, Department of Pediatrics, School of Medicine, University of California, Davis, CA

Marilyn K. Goldhaber, MPH, Perinatal Epidemiologist, Berkeley, CA, Triplet Mother

The Bookless children, Barrington, Rhode Island

The Triplet Connection

"A Network of Caring and Sharing for Multiple Birth Families"

Contact - The Triplet Connection
Phone (209) 474-0885, Fax (209) 474-9243
Email tc@tripletconnection.org Website www.tripletconnection.org

Informational Packets
Expectant Packets – includes the book, "Exceptional Pregnancies:
A Survival Guide to Parents Expecting Triplets or More"
Expectant Registration Packets – for those who already have the above book
New Parent Packets – those with new babies
(same as Expectant Packet without pregnancy information)
Tender Heart Packets – (for families dealing with a loss)

Newsletter
Quarterly issues wherein members and health professionals
share the joys and challenges of having and raising multiple
birth infants and children.

Clothing and Books
Books on pregnancy problems, NICU, raising children and a cookbook,
T-shirts, sweatshirts and other items.

Networking and Resources
Families who have "been there" and who are willing to share
their experiences with others.

A comprehensive directory of people who have dealt with different
issues within their families, and are available for help and support.

Database
The Triplet Connection maintains the world's largest database
of medical information pertaining to higher order multiple
pregnancy and birth.

The Shelton family, Pleasant Garden, North Carolina

What Professionals and Parents Say About "Exceptional Pregnancies"

W hat an incredible effort you have gone to in order to compile the most accurate information available for parents who are expecting twins, triplets or more. This information is vital to help educate prospective parents about the issues and problems of their very special pregnancies. As clearly stated in this manuscript, the care of multiple gestations must be different to accommodate the different problems posed by carrying more than one baby at a time. You clearly point out that the risks are real, but also that with a confident partnership between parents and physician the outcome will be as good as is humanly possible for each pregnancy. Parents must be empowered to be partners in their care, and accurate knowledge is the key to empowerment. This is the best accumulation of knowledge about multiple pregnancies that I have ever seen. I plan to use it with my patients. Many thanks to the authors for caring.

John Elliott, M.D.
Perinatologist and Specialist in High Order Multiple Pregnancies
Phoenix, Arizona

The completion of a triplet pregnancy and the parenting of the children is a major achievement for these exceptional families. Kathleen and Janet have outlined the various management alternatives in this guide and provided our patients with a superb and balanced resource to their many questions and concerns. It not only serves to educate them about the challenges ahead, but encourages them to be active participants in their care. This guide should be endorsed in all practices caring for these families in order to begin the dialogue that will lead to a team of educated parents and committed and attentive physicians.

Richard P. Porreco, M.D.
Maternal-Fetal and Reproductive Specialist Denver, Colorado

An outstanding job in developing a valuable resource for triplet families to be. Triplets are truly exceptional pregnancies, and mothers, families, physicians and the public need to know your "insider experience." The message cannot be emphasized enough that these are both exceptional and dangerous gestations, and that the best outcomes will require a partnership between both physicians and families. In order to be contributing partners, families need to have the kind of information that is found in the guide. I believe that the name "survival guide" is more appropriate than we know. Do I agree with every statement? No. But I agree with most of them, and more importantly I agree with the goal of educating patients so they can have knowledgeable discussions with their physicians, evaluate the information they receive from their physicians, and better understand the risks they face and the commitment that they will need to make to increase their chances of having a successful outcome. I look forward to the opportunity to share this guide with my multiple pregnancies.

Roger B. Newman, M.D.
Director, Maternal-Fetal Medicine
Medical University of South Carolina

At long last, the voice of experience is available for interested readers. Many books on the subject of triplets have been written by individuals with limited knowledge (one case, their own). In this case, the present authors draw on their collected experience with thousands of

triplet pregnancies. As an avid reader of the available material on triplet pregnancies I can state with certainty that this is *the* book to read.
There is nothing like it and certainly nothing better!

Louis Keith, M.D.
Professor, Dept. OBGYN
Northwestern Medical School, Chicago, IL

A must read for the newly diagnosed triplet (or greater) mother-
to-be. No other single source examines the issues of higher-order
multiples for parents. Beginning with the shock and joy of pregnancy
diagnosis, the guide skillfully addresses the significant and controversial areas of triplet pregnancy and pregnancy management and
empowers the triplet parent to know the issues. This guide will do
for expectant triplet moms what Dr. Spock's work did for parents in
the past 30 years.

J. Stephen Jones, M.D., Perinatologist
Greenville, South Carolina

"Exceptional Pregnancies" is a much needed and important resource for parents expecting triplets or more, and also for the medical team providing their care. The topics are discussed in an accurate and personal manner, and the information is based on vast experience with 19,000 families networked through the caring and sharing of "The Triplet Connection." I especially endorse the honest and
wise recommendations that the expectant parents seek out the most
experienced and qualified medical provider, along with assuring the
availability of a Level III Intensive Care Nursery. It is important that
the physician not only be expert, but also have a compassionate interest in this most important event. They must recognize the privi-
lege and responsibility of caring for expectant mothers of multiples
and their babies... with God's help! This book is a "must read," and
provides clear and accurate information that will help parents to be
compliant and to do whatever is necessary and best to promote a
successful outcome. It is not easy, but it is worth the struggle–and
you don't get a second chance!

Ronald E. Gunther, M.D., OBGYN
(Father of 19-year-old triplets)
McCall, Idaho

When I read your manuscript on twin and triplet pregnancy management, I couldn't help but think back to October of 1987 when my husband and I found we were expecting triplets. Frightened, anxious, hungry for information of any kind on the management of multiple gestations, we both did extensive searches of the literature. As physicians, we had access to whatever was then available, but were able to find little more than helpful tidbits such as the recommendation to rest more each day.

Fortunately, we did find out about The Triplet Connection and were sent the "skeleton" of what now appears in such completeness in "Exceptional Pregnancies." We devoured the information you sent us and let the information guide us, lead us, and help us through the entire, rather arduous pregnancy. With that information we were able to deliver three healthy 36-week gestation boys, each weighing more than 5 lbs.

"Exceptional Pregnancies" is a complete, detailed, well-grounded publication and guide. I can only hope that every Obstetrician, book store and library will have a copy of it on their shelves to offer parents who are searching for information!

Drs. Amy and Julio Alvarez
Orchard Park, NY
Parents of Triplets

"Exceptional and imperative information for anyone experiencing and managing a multiple pregnancy. As a mother of triplets, this is comprehensive, vital information I wish was available during my pregnancy."

Lisa Isola, Esq.
Mother of Triplets

I was delighted to read both versions ("A Survival Guide to Parents Expecting Triplets or More" and "A Survival Guide to Parents Expecting Twins") of "Exceptional Pregnancies." The authors relay important, lifesaving information in each of these guides that is complete and to the point, but also sensitive to the emotions of the reader.

Facing the challenges of a high-risk pregnancy can be difficult at best. I found the advice given in each manuscript to be practical and useful. Many families will benefit from these guides as they self educate and learn that they have some control towards a more positive pregnancy outcome. The resources supplied give the reader every opportunity to research all areas of multiple birth and pregnancy. The descriptions of various medical treatments are spelled out in an uncomplicated manner, making the information easy to understand. The definitions of medical terms help the patient know how to communicate their needs and better understand their health care providers.

I would hope that all OB/GYN physicians will recommend this guide to all parents expecting twins, triplets or more the moment their multiple pregnancies are diagnosed. How I wish this guide had been available to me during my own triplet pregnancy. This information WILL save lives!

Cheryl Bailey
Board Chairman, The Triplet Connection
(Mother of Triplets)

The Barrasso children, Long Island, New York

The Wallens, Anderson, Alabama

Introduction

> W hile the raising of trip-
> lets never gets easier, the joys are multiplied beyond
> the power of three.
>
> —SW in California (1)

> I remember when people used to know my name
> without adding, 'the one with triplets.'
>
> —EW in Illinois (2)

Every parent who has ever been told they are expecting multiples has an immediate, common bond with every other parent who
has received that same news. The initial reaction can include anything from exquisite joy to absolute terror.

While many multiple pregnancies are spontaneously conceived,
many more are fertility induced. Countless couples, after years of
frustration and disappointment because of their inability to have
children, are suddenly faced with the reality of being pregnant —

with far more than they bargained for!

Parents who are told they are expecting triplets, quadruplets or more are often urged to "reduce" their pregnancies by one or more fetuses to a more reasonable, manageable number. Fertility specialists, having done all they could to assist in the achievement of a much-wanted pregnancy, usher numb couples into geneticists' and high-risk pregnancy doctors' offices where they face a barrage of medical professionals, new terms, and a whole new world — the world of multiple births.

Is there *hope* for parents who find themselves expecting triplets, quadruplets, quintuplets or even more? Can they possibly expect to give birth to babies who will become healthy, normal children and adults? Are the risks to the mother overwhelming? If they do have a good outcome to their pregnancies, can they possibly take care of the physical, emotional and financial needs of babies born in "batches?"

These and thousands of other questions and concerns haunt the faces and tear at the hearts of every parent who enters the world of higher-multiple pregnancy. Gone are the dreams of carrying a "normal" pregnancy. Gone is the stability of everyday life. In its place is confusion borne of fear and information given by professionals who have never themselves experienced being a parent of three or more children simultaneously. Where can an expectant parent turn to find immediate answers and accurate information regarding higher-order multiple pregnancies? *Is* there hope for a healthy birth and a normal and enjoyable life after triplets or more? Is it important for an expectant parent to be informed in order to succeed?

If you're pregnant with triplets or more, we invite you to utilize both this book and The Triplet Connection organization fully to find clear and accurate information about your pregnancy and to help identify those things you can do to promote the best possible outcome. In other words, we *congratulate* you. We *welcome* you. We *understand* your concerns. We offer you information and resources which can be tremendously helpful to you now and in the future.

Triplets or more can be a joy and a miracle, worth all the effort they require. If you're going to succeed in carrying a triplet or larger multiple pregnancy, you're going to need to prepare to participate in helping to ensure a successful outcome. Your pregnancy will require hard work and commitment from both you and your physician.

We hope to make you aware of the fact that triplets or more are "do-able." They're definitely going to require more work and care during pregnancy and afterwards, but casual onlookers will never understand the rewards parents receive for the investment made. Every baby ever born is an absolute miracle. When you hold three or more babies in your arms, that miracle is only multiplied.

It is our hope and prayer that every parent who has the desire to do so can enjoy the miracle that countless thousands have enjoyed before them. We wish every expectant parent of multiples the very best possible outcome to their pregnancies, and we trust that this information will provide value and encouragement along the way.

Janet L. Bleyl and Kathleen S. Birch

The Kenney quadruplets, Summit, New Jersey

Endnotes

(1) The Triplet Connection Newsletter, 1994:Vol. 11.

(2) The Triplet Connection Newsletter, 1995:Vol. 12, No. 2, p.7.

The Deming family, Afton, Minnesota

The Journey Begins

Making an Informed Choice of Physicians

So, you've just found out that you're pregnant with triplets or more. Now what? After you've called all your family and friends to give them the news, you'll have some time to think. In the next months you will be incredibly involved with your pregnancy. After you deliver, you will look back and be amazed at what you've experienced and learned. But for right now, where do you begin?

One of the first and most important things to consider is choosing a physician. A higher-order multiple pregnancy requires the care of either an obstetrician or a perinatologist. What is the difference between the two? An obstetrician is a physician who has completed a four-year residency in Obstetrics and Gynecology. A perinatologist is a physician who has completed a four-year residency in Obstetrics and Gynecology and has then completed an additional two or three years of training in caring for high-risk pregnancies. A perinatologist's additional training gives him or her extensive experience managing high-risk pregnancies. An obstetrician has not had

2

additional training in high-risk pregnancies, but may still be qualified to follow your pregnancy. Some obstetricians may not be comfortable caring for a patient pregnant with higher-order multiples. In that case, you would expect the obstetrician to tell you. Likewise, you may not feel comfortable being followed by your obstetrician. If so, you should discuss this with your obstetrician and ask for a referral to a perinatologist.

The physician's experience is the most important factor to consider in your situation. If the obstetrician or perinatologist has not cared for at least ten or more patients who have successfully completed triplet pregnancies, he or she may not be your best choice. With quadruplet or quintuplet pregnancies, it is even more important not to be the first or second case your physician has followed. There is a learning curve for managing multiple pregnancies, and you do not want your physician to learn how to handle a multiple pregnancy at your expense.

How do you find a physician qualified to care for your pregnancy? If you were a fertility patient, your fertility clinic should be able to refer you to a perinatologist or obstetrician. If your pregnancy was a spontaneous higher-order multiple pregnancy or you are not comfortable with your fertility clinic's recommendations, you may have to do some checking around to find a physician with whom you're happy. A few places to start are:

- Ask your family doctor for a referral.
- Check with your local medical center to see if they can give you a recommendation.
- Check to see if your community has a physician referral service (look in the Yellow Pages of your telephone book or call your local hospital).
- Check to be sure your physician is board certified (see Appendix).
- Call your area's Level III Neonatal Intensive Care Unit (NICU). Because most small hospitals do not have a Level III NICU, you may need to check with your regional medical center. Neonatologists would typically be able to recommend a perinatologist or obstetrician.
- Call The Triplet Connection. Through our membership you may be able to network with other families in your area concerning their choice of physicians and their medical care.

After you choose a physician, you may want to make an appointment for a consultation to help you make the decision of whether or not to have him/her become your doctor.

If you live in a rural area and are unable to find a physician experienced with higher-order multiples, you may have to find an obstetrician who is willing to consult with an obstetrician or perinatologist who has experience with multiple pregnancies. You may even need to consider moving to find the quality of care you will need. This may sound drastic, but you have the rest of your life to relive a decision made on the basis of temporary inconvenience.

Your insurance company may limit your choice of physicians. When dealing with an insurance company, do not always take no for an answer if you wish to choose a physician who is not covered by your plan. Your request for a physician can sometimes be negotiated. Remember, in addition to three, four, or five lives at stake, there are literally hundreds of thousands of dollars at risk. Extending a high-risk pregnancy by two weeks is worth at least $3,000 *per day, per baby* (that's at least $126,000 in the case of triplets). Such information may be helpful in persuading your insurance company to consider your choice of physician.

> **Sometimes OB's are reluctant to look to experts for help. However, I must tell you about my doctor. He would have referred me to a specialist if the insurance company would have believed triplets were high-risk. They wanted to see trouble before I could be referred. With each appointment, he began, 'I talked to Dr. ...' Each week he had called the perinatologist.**
>
> **Although the insurance company would not pre-approve my delivery at the level III hospital, he reassured me that when the time came I would be admitted there 'as an emergency.' He discussed the suggestions given by The Triplet Connection with the perinatologist. I was on bedrest at four months, used home monitoring, and had Terbutaline available in case I needed it.**
>
> **At 36 weeks, with the perinatologist 'assisting,' he delivered my three healthy babies. He put aside his ego to put my babies first. . .**

2

Although he worried more than I did through-out the pregnancy, we worked as a team — resulting in a problem-free pregnancy and healthy babies. He deserves an award!

−SS in California(1)

When my water broke at 19 weeks, my doctor told me to go home and call back in 3 weeks if I was still pregnant. He said he didn't want to give me antibiotics because I might develop other infections later from drug resistance. He said it wouldn't do any good to use drugs to keep me from labor because they wouldn't help me this early anyway, and that they [the drugs] only work for two days. We were concerned, and my husband tried for three days to contact our doctor by phone. He wouldn't return our calls. Right now [at 20 weeks] I'm looking for a new physician."

Triplet Connection Member Letter

I was hospitalized when my water broke at 23 weeks gestation. My doctor told me that tocolytic drugs would only help for 24-48 hours, and it was too early to try to do anything. He induced labor, and each of my babies died by that night. I will always wonder whether they couldn't have done something to help me save my babies.

Triplet Connection Member
Medical Questionnaire Survey Response

In addition to finding a qualified physician, it is important to find a physician with whom you can communicate. Your physician should exhibit both competence and good common sense. He/she should be willing to listen to your concerns and respectfully respond to your wishes about the management of your pregnancy. A positive rapport and effective communication with your physician and his/her health care team is critical. The success of your pregnancy may depend on it.

Keep in mind that most obstetricians and perinatologists have very busy practices. Sometimes they may need a gentle reminder to take a few extra minutes to discuss questions or concerns that you have about your pregnancy. Many physicians routinely allow more time for their patients with high-risk pregnancies. If yours doesn't and you feel like you need more time for questions, ask about scheduling a little more time for your next appointment. If you still feel too rushed at your regular appointments, you may want to schedule a consultation with your physician. This consultation can be a scheduled time for you and your spouse to sit down and talk with your physician, and it may become a valuable turning point in the patient/physician relationship.

Choosing and working well with your physician will make your pregnancy easier. It is important that you, your partner, and any other support person who interacts with your physician always remains courteous, patient, and willing to listen and work with your physician. You will expect to be treated with respect, and your physician should be treated respectfully as well. A high-risk pregnancy is often a high-stress pregnancy. Don't let your fears and the stress of your pregnancy interfere with a good rapport with your physician. If either you or your physician feels alienated, you will not work together effectively.

If you feel uncomfortable with the response you receive from your physician, it may be necessary to find another physician. This is best done early in the pregnancy. Watch for the warning signs. Does your physician return your calls? Does he/she welcome your questions and answer them? Is he/she readily available? Is his/her staff willing to relay your concerns and messages without running unnecessary "interference" so that your physician is not "bothered" (and is sometimes unaware)? Do you get the feeling that your pregnancy management is being handled as a special case (it *is* both special and high-risk, you know)?

If you find that you are in need of changing physicians, where do you turn? If you truly feel that you are receiving inadequate care, it is time to get an informed second (or third) opinion. If there are other physicians locally to whom you feel you can turn for advice, talk with them about the care you are receiving. Ask around. Talk with friends, family, and others about physicians who may be particularly helpful and successful. If there is no one locally to whom you feel you can turn, contact The Triplet Connection or other resources for help. Remember, you may need to relocate temporarily in order to obtain excellent care. Do not feel that this is impossible. Your babies' lives may depend upon what you do at a time like this.

Talking to Your Physician with Confidence

There are a few things that will help you have a productive conversation with your physician. First, identify your questions and concerns. If you have specific questions, you may want to write them down – then you won't become distracted and for get them. Writing down questions also helps you to organize your thoughts beforehand so that you can speak clearly and confidently. Second, assert yourself in a friendly manner. Your physician may be behind schedule and in a hurry, but you may have limited chances to talk with him/her so you may need to be prepared to take advantage of each opportunity. If your physician does not have time to answer all your questions immediately, it may be best to schedule a consultation as mentioned above. That way, your physician may not feel as rushed, and you may feel more on "equal ground" sitting in his/her office in street clothes rather than in an exam room in a hospital gown.

It is important to educate yourself about your pregnancy so that you can discuss medical issues with your physician. You will feel more confident, and your physician will probably respect you for taking the time to learn about your pregnancy. However, if something comes up in your pregnancy that you don't understand, ask about it. It is critical that you remain informed.

It's in everyone's best interest to keep a positive rapport between patient and physician. If you have a difference of opinion with your physician about your care, first try discussing that difference with him/her. Maybe one or both of you have misunderstood the situation. You and your physician may disagree on some issues (use of home uterine activity monitoring, weight gain, or activity during pregnancy, for example), but you must be satisfied with the final outcome. It's worth working with your physician to come to a satisfactory decision. The following situation is a good example:

One couple found themselves working with a very well educated, experienced specialist who was firmly against home uterine activity monitoring, was in favor of restricted weight gain, and was opposed

> to bedrest. After weeks of disagreement, the couple tried a new approach. They set up an appointment to talk with their physician. They began by stating that while they certainly appreciated her input, education, and years of experience, they needed to consider many sources in order to make a truly educated decision. They listed the resources that they had already utilized to learn about triplet pregnancies. They stated that they felt certain things (such as an adequate diet, bedrest and home monitoring) were safety issues, and therefore non-negotiable. At that point, the doctor was satisfied that the couple had made truly informed choices, and graciously agreed to support their decision! (2)
>
> The Triplet Connection Newsletter

One word of caution: patient education is especially important during a higher-order multiple pregnancy, but as a patient (or spouse) it is also important to recognize your physician's training and expertise. Your physician may recommend care (or decline treatment options) during your pregnancy which may initially appear unacceptable to you. Take time to listen and discuss issues with your physician. You may not understand all aspects that your physician is considering. We expect our physicians to be open to our questions and expectations, and we must also be open to theirs. The key is to have a good rapport established so that *as a team* you may work to have the healthiest pregnancy possible.

> I live in an area where there are no high-risk doctors, and my doctor believed that triplets were 'just like twins, only one more.' He was so wrong. I didn't find out that I was having triplets until my 18th week because my doctor didn't think sonograms were necessary even though I had been on fertility drugs. I was gaining too much weight, and I was sicker than a dog. A week after I was hospitalized for preterm labor, my water broke. I was 31 weeks

2

at that point. I was flown to a larger city with a high-risk facility . . . I felt so much better after I had arrived at the high-risk facility. These people knew what they were doing. I was able to relax instead of worrying about everything . . .

The Triplet Connection Newsletter

The Beeson children, La Jolla, California

Endnotes

(1) The Triplet Connection Newsletter, 1995:Vol 12, No 4, p. 11.

(2) The Triplet Connection Newsletter, 1994:Vol 11, No 1, p.12-13.

Choosing a Birthplace

Location for Delivery of Your Triplets

Where to deliver your triplets may seem a ridiculous consideration. A hospital is a hospital, right? The services a hospital may offer vary greatly, usually due to the size of the hospital and the population it serves. A major concern with the hospital you will be delivering your triplets at is the type of nurseries it offers. There are three types of hospital nurseries: Levels I, II and III. This breakdown of nurseries is standard throughout the United States.

A Level I nursery is a "standard" nursery found at all hospitals that deliver babies. The Level I nursery serves low-risk patients (healthy newborns born at or near term without any complications). Your local community hospital will have a Level I nursery if that hospital delivers babies.

A step up from the Level I nursery is the Level II nursery. This nursery is designed to meet the medical needs of newborns with moderate risks and complications. Level II nurseries also take care of the "feed and grow" newborns (babies that just need some addi-

2

tional time to be fed and to grow before being sent home). They also take care of babies who may need routine monitoring due to prematurity or other complications.

The third type of nursery is the Level III nursery. Level III nurseries are Neonatal Intensive Care Units (NICUs). These nurseries are designed to meet the needs of infants born with conditions or complications that require close and constant monitoring. The NICU cares for infants who need help breathing, who are very preterm, who are low birthweight, or who have any other serious complications such as cardiac or respiratory problems that require constant monitoring and care.

If you're pregnant with triplets or more you should plan your delivery to be at a hospital with a Level III NICU. A Level III nursery is equipped to meet the special needs that triplets may have. These care requirements are sometimes unexpected and require immediate response, and an emergency hospital transfer for such unexpected conditions may be hazardous. A triplet delivery at a hospital with only a Level I nursery would not be recommended. It would be a tragedy to lose your preterm babies because they were born at the wrong hospital. A Level II nursery *may be* adequate, but triplets *often* need care that only a Level III nursery can provide.

One warning about Level II nurseries. There is an alarming movement in some community hospitals to meet the requirements to provide a Level II nursery. Technically, they are meeting the requirements, but that does not mean that the expertise and experience is there to meet the unique medical needs of a higher-order multiple birth. If your local community hospital is small and has a Level II nursery, you will want to check with the hospital to find out how long they've had a Level II nursery, how much experience they have with preterm babies and whether they have in-house, round-the-clock care provided by a neonatologist (a physician who is a specialist in caring for newborns, particularly high-risk newborns), rather than just on-call coverage by a pediatrician or neonatologist. Some small hospitals boasting a Level II nursery, in reality, should only be a Level I nursery. Often, they do not even have a neonatologist on staff, nor does the nursing staff have experience or training to care for very preterm infants (both *very* important considerations).

Unfortunately, politics and finances often dictate the recommendation to a hospital that is ill equipped to handle the possible complications of multiple birth. At times parents are led to believe that certain hospitals are adequate, when in reality there is a much better facility nearby.

When talking with your physician, be sure to ask him/her about what level nursery is available in your area. Take the time to set up a tour through each nursery (Level I, II, III). The unfamiliar medical surroundings may be overwhelming initially. Seeing these nurseries in operation prior to having *your* babies in them will help prepare you for the time when your babies will be hospitalized. It may also be a good time to talk to a neonatologist and/or NICU nurse about preterm babies and their care. This experience will definitely help you realize the importance of doing everything possible to help prevent extremely preterm birth.

In rural areas, you may have to travel some distance to have the use of a Level II or Level III nursery. If that's your situation, be sure to discuss that issue with your physician. You may end up having to spend the last few weeks of your pregnancy away from home to be near a larger medical center.

It is important for you to know that some medical centers and their affiliated physicians have established (informally or formally) *protocols* for treatment of pregnancy complications. For example, some medical group practices and/or hospitals may not treat preterm labor prior to 24 weeks gestation. Even later in pregnancy, they may be unwilling to attempt interventions which may be risky or aggressive in order to try to salvage what may at first seem a hopeless complication. (An example would be aggressively working to save the subsequent babies if one were born extremely prematurely–trying to hold off delivery until the other babies would have a better chance of survival. Another example would be aggressively working to prevent infection and labor in the case of premature rupture of membranes.) While some physicians will aggressively treat such complications, even early in pregnancy, others will do nothing (allowing the pregnancy to miscarry rather than having to treat difficult complications and/or face the possibility of extremely preterm infants). They may send a patient home following serious complications, and will not treat her unless or until she reaches a certain number of weeks gestation (with the assumption that the pregnancy will likely miscarry). Due to protocol, some physicians will make no resuscitation efforts should a baby be born prior to a given number of weeks gestation (i.e. 24 weeks) when there may have been a chance of healthy survival with aggressive medical intervention.

Prior to choosing your physician and your delivery hospital, find out what their protocols are in regard to medical intervention in the event that you should develop complications early in pregnancy.

I checked into the two hospitals in our community and was horrified to find that one of them would not treat me for preterm labor unless I was at least 24 weeks gestation. The other hospital would treat me for preterm labor at my doctor's request at any time. I ended up being treated in the hospital from 19 weeks when my water broke until I delivered at 31 weeks.

<u>The Triplet Connection</u> -
Medical Questionnaire Survey Response

The Adams children, Thomasville, Georgia

Educating Yourself

$\mathcal{A}$t the time I received your literature, I was about 16 weeks along in my healthy pregnancy with triplets . . . We were very excited about the arrival of our triplets, but that excitement was mixed with a lot of trepidation. Much of that anxiety was due to simply being unaware of what to expect . . . We are [now] much more knowledgeable and feel so much more prepared for the adventure ahead of us.

–ED in Germany (1)

Once you've found a physician to follow your pregnancy and you know what types of nurseries are available in your area, what's next? There are a few things you will want to learn about your care during your pregnancy. Much of the information in the upcoming chapters is basic information which may become very important to you. This information will help you educate yourself so that you can have the best possible pregnancy outcome. Other information is specific to the special needs of a higher-order multiple pregnancy, and can also be invaluable to you.

Here's a list of topics that you need to be well aware of:

• Multi-Fetal Pregnancy Reduction
• Nutrition During Multiple Pregnancy
• Multiple Pregnancy Management
• Preterm Labor: Recognition, Treatment, Prevention
• Home Uterine Activity Monitoring
• Self Monitoring for Contractions
• Bedrest During Pregnancy
• Preventing Preterm Birth
• Managing Preterm Labor
• General Tips for Pregnant Moms
• Possible Complications of Pregnancy
• Breast Feeding Triplets
• Bringing Babies Home (Yes! They're Yours to Take Care Of!)
• For Safety's Sake
• Enjoying the Miracle

Some of the information contained in these chapters may seem overwhelming and/or negative. Please bear in mind that being aware of *potential* problems or complications can often pay rich dividends! You may be able to *avoid* many problems if you are aware of those things which can be done to promote the healthiest pregnancy possible.

Your ability to be as knowledgeable as possible during your pregnancy may make an invaluable difference in outcome. You may be able to recognize signs or symptoms that would otherwise go undetected in time to stop the progress of potentially dangerous conditions. By becoming well informed you may be able to alert your physician to possible alternatives or discuss new information which can sometimes make a tremendous difference in the outcome of your pregnancy.

Endnotes

(1) The Triplet Connection Newsletter, 1996:Vol. 13, No. 4, p.26.

The Brody family, Binghamton, New York

Multi-Fetal Pregnancy Reduction

My advice to anyone con-
sidering selective reduction would be to get all the
facts, then get some more. Also, I would definitely
talk to someone who has been there. Remember, this
decision never goes away. (1)

The Triplet Connection Newsletter

With the increased number of pregnancies due to the use of fertility drugs, we're also seeing a spiraling number of higher-order
multiple pregnancies. With this increase, more medical and ethical
considerations are surfacing. One such issue is reducing the number
of fetuses in the pregnancy (termed "multi-fetal pregnancy reduction," MFPR). MFPR is a procedure in which one or more fetuses are
terminated, leaving the pregnancy with fewer fetuses to grow and
develop. For example, a triplet pregnancy may be reduced to a twin
pregnancy or a quadruplet pregnancy may be reduced to a triplet or
twin pregnancy. The number of fetuses terminated may vary.

The topic of MFPR has many considerations, both medical and
ethical. The issue of fetal reduction is tremendously difficult for many
couples to face. Ironically, infertile couples who have longed for a

pregnancy and for children are sometimes faced with the consideration of terminating at least one fetus in their pregnancy.

The Triplet Connection does not recommend whether a couple should or shouldn't have an MFPR. This is a very delicate and personal decision, and we empathize with those who are faced with such a decision. Many couples who call The Triplet Connection are concerned, feeling that they are being pressured to have a fetal reduction when they really want to carry their higher-order multiple pregnancies — but are afraid to do so based on what their physicians are telling them. We want to make sure that couples are fully informed when they make their decision. This is a crucial decision which lasts a lifetime, and you must learn all you can in order to make the best decision for yourself and your family.

Couples may receive conflicting opinions from different physicians regarding MFPR. Some physicians recommend the procedure liberally for higher-order multiple pregnancies, with the opinion that the patient will be more likely to have a successful pregnancy outcome carrying fewer fetuses. Other physicians are not convinced that reducing the number of fetuses improves the outcome in higher-order multiple pregnancies. Some physicians are convinced that pregnancies which have been reduced carry a greater potential for prematurity than those which are left alone. Most physicians acknowledge that some of the risks associated with reduction can cause complications resulting in loss of the entire pregnancy, yet carrying a higher-order multiple pregnancy (without fetal reduction) also poses risks.

We at The Triplet Connection are alarmed when we hear from couples who are told that the *only* way to successfully carry their higher-order multiple pregnancy is to reduce the pregnancy to at least twins. One basic question for many couples may be whether an MFPR improves the outcome of a higher-order multiple pregnancy. Studies have been conducted to determine this, with conflicting conclusions drawn. More research is currently being conducted. Couples contemplating MFPR must also face a myriad of emotional issues. While some couples are comfortable with the decision to reduce the pregnancy, many couples will grieve the loss of the fetus(es). Sometimes this grieving occurs immediately, but more often there is unexpected grieving following the birth of the remaining babies. The emotional aspects of MFPR should be thoroughly discussed and contemplated before any decision is made. Your physician may not be

2

in the best position to discuss many of the aspects of MFPR. You may want to consider talking with a psychiatrist, psychologist or counselor. Through The Triplet Connection you can connect with many other families who have undergone an MFPR or those who have not, who are willing to share their experiences with you.

If a couple is considering MFPR, they should extensively discuss the medical aspects of carrying a higher-order multiple pregnancy as well as the medical aspects of an MFPR with a physician. It may be best to talk to a physician who routinely performs MFPR, and also to one who successfully follows patients pregnant with higher-order multiples who have chosen not to reduce their pregnancies. A physician who sees many patients pregnant with multiples may be able to give you both the pros and cons of MFPR, but you may still want to get a second (or third) opinion. Again, you may wish to discuss the issue with others who have reduced their pregnancies, and also with others who have decided against the procedure.

The procedure of MFPR carries risks, the major complication being the loss of the entire pregnancy. In addition, many couples believe that once their pregnancy has been reduced they are in the same lower-risk category of a twin pregnancy (if reduced to two). Unfortunately, this does not appear to be the case. Reduced pregnancies, for whatever reason, often result in preterm birth. The risks of reduced pregnancies are not fully understood, but it should be made clear to patients that there are inherent risks for the remaining fetuses after MFPR. Reduced pregnancies should still be considered high-risk pregnancies.

There are a couple of studies that discuss the difference between carrying a triplet pregnancy and a twin pregnancy. (2,3) These studies seem to indicate that triplet pregnancies can be just as successful as twin pregnancies; however, more "effort" is required to have a successful triplet pregnancy outcome. One study notes that preterm labor occurred more often in triplet pregnancies than in twin pregnancies. (3) In this study preterm labor occurred in 40% of twin pregnancies and 80% of triplet pregnancies. In summary, a triplet pregnancy may be as successful as a twin pregnancy, but a triplet pregnancy requires a dedicated physician and health care team to more closely manage, detect, and address potential medical complications. It also requires a patient being very educated, motivated, and willing to work very hard to achieve success.

With the increased use of fertility drugs there has been an increase in the number of quadruplet and quintuplet pregnancies. Women pregnant with quadruplets or quintuplets may be pressured very strongly to reduce their pregnancies because their physicians feel that the entire pregnancy will be lost without MFPR. Once again, this decision must be made by the couple and should be well thought out. If you choose to carry a quadruplet (or greater) pregnancy, you will be heartened to know that perinatologists are becoming more experienced and successful in managing quadruplet and quintuplet pregnancies. All of the physicians on The Triplet Connection Scientific Advisory Board, as well as *many* others, have successfully managed quadruplet and quintuplet pregnancies. In May of 1993, a mother in Indiana successfully carried sextuplets and delivered her babies at 30 weeks gestation. All of the babies were healthy. Two more full sets of healthy sextuplets were born in subsequent years. Though rare, healthy septuplet births (seven babies) are now occurring. In November of 1997 septuplets were born in Iowa, and in the following two months two additional sets of septuplets were delivered in Saudi Arabia. In December of 1998 a family in Texas gave birth to octuplets (8 babies) with one baby dying.

No one looks at higher-order multiple pregnancies which happen as a result of fertility drugs or procedures as being an "optimal" result of those drugs or procedures. As the science of infertility treatment and monitoring progresses, there will be fewer higher-multiple pregnancies (particularly quadruplets and greater multiples) resulting from fertility assistance. Statistically, for the number of women currently seeking medical intervention to solve infertility problems, higher-multiple pregnancies are rare. However, statistics mean nothing when you find yourself facing a higher-multiple pregnancy; for you, the statistic is 100%.

If you are pregnant with triplets, quadruplets, quintuplets or more and feel you are being pressured into having an MFPR, please contact a physician experienced in following larger multiple pregnancies. If you are unable to find a physician with this experience, please call The Triplet Connection for help in locating an experienced physician for you to talk with.

If faced with the decision of having an MFPR, please take time to make the choice that's right for you. This decision lasts a lifetime, and all aspects of such a critical issue need to be thoroughly considered.

Couples who have an MFPR often lose touch with The Triplet

Connection. If you decide to have an MFPR, *please* stay in contact. Your pregnancy is still high risk, and we may have information that could be helpful to you. Also, we would appreciate your contribution of information through your medical questionnaire.

It is our hope that every family who must face this extremely difficult decision will avail themselves of the best possible information, and we are here to help in any way we can.

The Dilley sextuplets, Berne, Indiana

Endnotes

(1)*The Triplet Connection Newsletter*, 1996:Vol 13, No. 1, p.14. *(Mother of Reduced Pregnancy Triplets)*.

(2) Porreco RP, Burke MS, Hendrix ML. *Multifetal Reduction of Triplets and Pregnancy Outcome. Obstet & Gynecol 1991;78:3:1:335-339.*

(3) Melgar CA, Rosenfeld DL, et al. *Perinatal Outcome After Multifetal Reduction to Twins Compared With Nonreduced Multiple Gestation. Obstet & Gynecol 1991;78:5:763-767.*

The Hall children, Augusta, Georgia

Taking Care of You and Your Babies

Nutrition During Multiple Pregnancy

Good nutrition is one of the most important considerations during a multiple pregnancy. Healthy eating will help ensure a successful pregnancy with the birth of healthy babies. Careful attention to nutrition has a greater capacity to influence birth weight in multiple pregnancies than in singleton pregnancies. In singleton pregnancies the ultimate birth weight is influenced as much by genetics as by modified environmental factors such as nutrition. However, in multiple pregnancies, the limitation on growth caused by uterine crowding makes the influence of factors such as nutrition and cessation of smoking more important.

Weight Gain

Higher-order multiple pregnancies are most successful when the mother eats enough food to adequately support the pregnancy. The specific aspects of nutrition that contribute to infant health and well being include total weight gain, pattern of weight gain, good quality eating habits, and nutrient supplements during pregnancy.

Weight gain information from respondents to The Triplet Connection medical questionnaire indicated that normal-weight women who gained 45-70 pounds carried their babies longer, felt better throughout their pregnancies, and delivered much larger, healthier babies than those born at equal gestational ages where the mother had a lesser weight gain. With *rare* exceptions, women who gained less than 35 pounds delivered prematurely. (1) Women who unexpectedly delivered early had babies who did much better if the mother had adequate weight gain up until the time of their preterm delivery.

3

The amount of weight gain recommended will vary somewhat depending on a woman's pre-pregnancy weight. Underweight women should be encouraged to gain more weight, while overweight women may not need to gain as much. Both situations (underweight or overweight) pose unique challenges. Underweight women are at increased risk of delivering preterm, low-birthweight babies. Overweight women may have poor eating habits and are at greater risk of developing gestational diabetes. Both situations require healthier eating during pregnancy, and consultation with a nutritionist may be helpful. Attempting to lose or maintain weight, even if you're overweight, is **never** recommended during a higher-order multiple pregnancy.

Assessing your nutritional state is important for all women who are pregnant, and is especially important for a woman pregnant with multiples. Your caloric requirements increase dramatically with a multiple pregnancy. However, trying to count calories is ineffective, especially when no one really knows how many extra calories a woman pregnant with multiples really requires. Monitoring and maintaining appropriate weight gain during your pregnancy is usually a better indication that you are meeting your nutritional requirements than trying to count calories.

Rate of Weight Gain

The **rate** of weight gain is also important. Women with a low rate of weight gain are more than twice as likely to deliver prematurely compared to those with a higher rate of weight gain. (2) In twin pregnancies, a higher rate of weight gain is associated with greater infant birth weight and longer gestation. (3) Weight gain and rate of weight gain work hand in hand to help promote a healthy pregnancy.

A study by Luke, et. al. gives a recommendation of 44 pounds total weight for **twin** pregnancies at a rate of about one pound per week for the first 24 weeks of pregnancy, and recommends a weight gain of 1.25 pounds per week for the remainder of the pregnancy. (4) There are currently no official recommendations for weight gain with triplet pregnancies. However, analysis of data from 1,138 surveys of triplet mothers has allowed researchers to conclude "it seems reasonable to recommend weight gain of 36 lbs by 24 weeks, and a rate of gain of 1.25 pounds per week thereafter for triplet gestations."(5)

Professional Resources for Individual Care

Registered dietitians (R.D.s) are nutrition experts who can be invaluable resources for you during your multiple pregnancy. In choosing an R.D. for your multiple pregnancy it is important to locate an R.D. who has specific experience in perinatal nutrition. Ask the R.D. if he/she is a member of the Perinatal Nutrition Dietetic Practice Group of The American Dietetic Association. This group of professionals specializes in high-risk pregnancy care. Continued consultation with an R.D. throughout your pregnancy is encouraged. As your pregnancy progresses, your appetite, tolerance for foods, digestive process and nutritional needs will change, and so will the challenges of maintaining healthy eating during your pregnancy. Your dietitian can address those needs, modify your nutritional program, and work with your physician to ensure that your nutritional needs are met.

Many insurance companies will cover consultations by an R.D. with referral from your physician. If such a consultation is not covered by your insurance carrier, you may consider seeing an R.D. at your own expense. Patients on public assistance should seek help from the dietitian at the Maternal and Child Health Program or the WIC (Women, Infants and Children) programs.

Although the WIC program is not designed to provide comprehensive medical nutrition therapy, especially for high-risk pregnancies, it does provide basic services such as breastfeeding education, nutrition education, and helps provide nutritious foods. WIC can also help women learn how to receive adequate health care and obtain referrals to other social programs and services. WIC is not designed to replace the nutritional recommendations given by a physician or R.D., but it certainly can help those struggling to meet their prescribed nutrition plan. Ask your physician about a WIC referral.

Healthy Eating

What type of diet is best for you? Every woman's situation and nutritional needs are different, so it's difficult to recommend a set diet. Again, it would be worth your time to have your physician give you a referral to see a registered dietitian, preferably one who specializes in perinatal/obstetrical nutrition. If your physician is unable to give you a referral, call The American Dietetic Association (1-800-366-1655 or 1-800-877-1600).

There is no "one and only" way to eat for a healthy multiple pregnancy. You have many options for healthy eating. The clinical dietitian can discuss those options with you. You may have many questions about nutrition, and your R.D. is qualified to discuss your concerns and answer your questions. Topics in an individual nutrition plan include recommendations for weight gain, nutrient supplements, meal/snack frequency and food choices. Registered dietitians are also trained to devise medical nutrition therapies for specific complications such as hyperemesis (excessive vomiting), diabetes, gestational diabetes, etc.

Your physician may also have nutritional information available for you or may have someone in his/her office who is designated to provide nutritional counseling. There are also different nutritional guides available, such as on the following pages.

Smoking, Alcohol and Drug Use.

Countless studies have shown that smoking, drinking alcohol and using drugs are unhealthy for fetal and maternal health. Any caring parent will want to discontinue use of harmful substances of any kind for the health and well being of their children. Use of over-the-counter medications should also be checked thoroughly with your physician before use. Substances as seemingly harmless as cough syrup have recently been linked to serious birth defects. Excessive caffeine consumption is also known to be harmful during pregnancy.

Any mother who may have had a long history of smoking, alcohol consumption, etc., should now be prompted, as never before, to make life changes for the sake of her unborn children. If help is needed to achieve a smoking-free/drug-free pregnancy, seek professional counseling to ensure your childrens' health.

Daily Food Guide for Pregnant Women
Adjusted for Triplet Pregnancies

Food Group	Amounts of food that make up one serving	Number of servings daily	Hints for planning meals
Milk and Milk products	1 cup of whole milk 1-1/2 oz. of cheese 1-1/3 cups of cottage cheese 1 cup of plain yogurt 1-1/2 cups ice cream	6	6 glasses of milk (8 oz. each) or 3 oz. cheese and 4 glasses of milk
Protein Foods: Animal (2 serv.) Vegetable (2 serv.)	1 cup dried beans, cooked 2 eggs 1/2 cup of tuna 1/4 cup of peanut butter 2 oz. of beef fish or chicken 1/2 cup nuts	5	Eat regular meals. DO NOT SKIP MEALS!
Breads and Cereals	1 slice of whole wheat bread 1/2 cup cooked cereal 3/4 cup cold cereal 1 corn tortilla 1/2 cup of rice, noodles or pasta 6 saltine crackers	8	Eat as snacks several times each day.
Dark Green Vegetables	1 cup raw 3/4 cup cooked such as broccoli, spinach, asparagus, cabbage, romaine lettuce, collards, kale, brussel sprouts	2	Twice a day
Vitamin C Fruits and Vegetables	1 cup raw strawberries, kiwi or mango 1/2 cup of orange or grapefruit juice 1 medium fruit or vegetable	2	At least 2 servings per day.
Other Fruits and vegetables	1 cup raw iceberg lettuce 3/4 cup potato 1 medium fruit or vegetable such as squash, carrots, banana, apple, grapes, corn, etc.	As many servings as you would like.	

Adapted from a nutrition guide for pregnant women developed by Ventura County Health Department. Revisions for the Triplet Pregnancy by Erica Gunderson, M.S., M.P.H., R.D., November 1987.

Daily Menu Guidelines
For Expectant Mothers of Multiples

Food Group	Serving Size	Non-Pregnant	Single-ton	Twin	Triplet	Quad
Dairy	8 oz. (1c.) milk 8 oz. (1 c.) cottage cheese (calcium fortified) 8 oz. (1 c.) ice cream 1 slice (1 oz.) hard cheese	4	6	8	10	12
Meats, Fish, Poultry	1 oz.	6	6	10	10	12
Eggs	1 fresh	–	1	2	2	2
Vegetables	1/2 cup or 1 fresh	4	4	4	5	6
Fruits	1/2 cup or 1 fresh	4	4	7	8	8
Grains, Bread	1 oz. (3/4 cup) cooked grain or 1 slice bread	8	8	10	12	12
Fats, oils, and nuts	1 Tbsp. oil 1 pat butter 1 oz. nuts	4	5	6	7	8

3

Used with permission from:
When You're Expecting Twins, Triplets, or Quads, by Barbara Luke and Tamara Eberlein©
1999 HarperCollins

Daily Food Guide – Usual Diet Intake

Write down everything you had to eat or drink from the time you got up in the morning until you went to bed at night. Indicate the amount of the food/drink, how it was prepared and the time the item was ingested.

Meals and Snacks		Description of Food Items				Food Group Check List					
Time	Place	Food/Drink	Amount	Preparation	Milk Product	Protein	Bread/ Grains	Dark Gr. Veg.	Vit C F/V	Other F/V	

Prenatal Vitamins

Prenatal vitamins are part of a well-balanced multiple pregnancy nutrition plan. It is important to have a prenatal vitamin that includes folic acid. A folic acid supplement before and during the first few weeks of pregnancy decreases the risk of having a child born with spina bifida (an open spine). Your physician will prescribe a prenatal vitamin. Be sure to take them as directed. In addition, most women pregnant with multiples will not receive adequate iron in their diets even with a supplemental prenatal vitamin. Most physicians will prescribe a supplemental iron tablet. Iron is absorbed best with orange juice, grapefruit juice or lemonade (citrus drinks), and absorbs poorly with milk or tea. Some women do not tolerate oral iron tablets, but there are a number of different iron preparations designed to reduce gastrointestinal upset. Remember to keep all prenatal vitamins out of the reach of children, as they can be toxic in large amounts.

Hydration

An important part of your nutrition plan includes the amount of fluids you are drinking. Dehydration can be a serious condition during your multiple pregnancy, since it may lead to preterm labor. If you become dehydrated, your body's blood volume drops and uterine contractions may follow. Therefore, it is important that you get enough fluids. How much is enough? Most dietitians recommend 5-6 (8 oz.) servings of milk per day for a mother expecting triplets. Milk is 87.4% water, so hydration with milk, then fruit juice (which also provides added nourishment and water), and then water may be a much better plan than just relying on water for hydration. Other sources of fluids are fresh fruits (watermelon, melons, grapes, oranges, citrus fruits) and soups. Sport drinks may also be a better alternative for hydration than just plain water.

Drinking large volumes of water may not be your best choice. With a growing pregnancy, you will feel "full" even without drinking large amounts of water. This feeling can cause a loss of appetite at a time when it's critical to eat greater amounts of healthy food.

Milk is the best source of water and nourishment available and contains proteins, vitamins, minerals, and other nutrients. As pregnancy progresses and you begin to experience the sensation of being "filled up quickly," it may be a good idea to forego fluids at meal time so that you can take more solid nutrition. After eating and between meals, drink a nutritious beverage. Eat and drink only nourishing foods and fluids! At this time, you must be sure that everything eaten is nourishing to you and your babies. Limit or delete empty calorie foods and drinks! The recommendation to drink large quantities of water per day just because of concern over preterm labor is short-sighted, and this liquid intake should be considered as part of your overall nutrition plan.

Even when you've committed to healthy eating during your pregnancy, it may still be frustrating to maintain a healthy eating regime. At the beginning of your pregnancy, nausea and vomiting may make weight gain difficult. At the end of your pregnancy the size of your uterus will crowd your stomach, which decreases your appetite (and may cause heartburn and makes eating a chore). Late in pregnancy, eating sometimes causes hyperventilation, as the lungs become compressed due to added pressure from the expanded stomach. Again, an R.D. can work with you to modify your nutrition plan as your pregnancy progresses. Remember, adequate weight gain is important for a healthy pregnancy. You are eating for four (or more)!

Salt

Salt is an essential nutrient, and it is dangerous for you to become too low in sodium, particularly during pregnancy when there is actually an increased need for salt due to the extra demands being placed on the mother's body. Salt is responsible for aiding heart action, brain function, kidney function, adrenal function, the nervous system, the body's regulation of blood and amniotic fluid volume, and efficient action of muscles. Lack of salt can lead to arm and leg cramps, easy fatigability, weakness, headaches, dizziness, decreased appetite, rise in blood pressure, decreased blood volume (which can trigger premature labor), and can even cause convulsions.

Sodium is required in pregnancy for the expanded maternal tissue and fluid compartments as well as to provide for fetal needs. The normal patient should use the level of sodium she prefers, and routine sodium restriction during pregnancy is *not advised.*

Nausea and Vomiting

Some pregnant women have severe nausea, while others will have little or none. Nausea and vomiting generally occur by the sixth week of gestation and subside around the twelfth week. There is some indication that high hormone levels during pregnancy may cause nausea and vomiting. If this is the case, it would make sense that triplet pregnancies would have more nausea and vomiting since hormonal levels are higher in multiple pregnancies. Whatever the reason, nausea and vomiting may make your pregnancy (particularly the early weeks) miserable.

3

Hyperemesis

Sometimes what begins as nausea and occasional vomiting progresses to a more serious condition known as hyperemesis. This is a condition which often requires hospitalization to administer intravenous therapy to prevent (or treat) dehydration. Occasionally, an expectant mother does not seem to recover from this condition sufficiently, and she will require intravenous feedings in order to sustain her own health and the well-being of her babies. Such a condition is extremely hard on an expectant mother.

Total parenteral nutrition (TPN) is a means of providing nutrition through intravenous "feeding." This is used when severe hyperemesis is preventing the pregnant woman from receiving adequate nutrition. TPN provides necessary nutrition until the severe hyperemesis is under control and the patient is able to consume enough nutrients by mouth or by placement of a gastro-intestinal tube (a tube going from the nose down the throat to the stomach).

Networking with others who have undergone a similar experience and have had a good outcome with their pregnancies can be of tremendous benefit. If you should find yourself diagnosed with hyperemesis, be sure to contact The Triplet Connection for networking information. Hang in there! You will get through this!

Suggestions to help with nausea and vomiting:

- Avoid eating greasy and/or spicy foods.
- A protein snack (i.e. milk, cottage cheese, yogurt) at night may help.
- Do not let your stomach become empty!
- Keep crackers with you (and at your bedside) to eat when nausea strikes. Eating crackers before rising may help.
- Eat several small meals or snacks throughout the day rather than three large meals. This keeps food in the stomach at all times.
- Low blood sugar may cause nausea. Try eating carbohydrates (i.e. fresh fruits, breads, cereals) as a rapid source of blood glucose.
- Drink milk or juice between meals rather than with meals.
- Brush your teeth later in the day.
- Spearmint, peppermint or raspberry leaf tea may help settle an upset stomach (mint is a natural anti-nausea source). *Note: Mint is also known to be a mild stimulant, so beware of any increased uterine activity or contractions which could possibly be associated with consumption of mint.*
- Sucking on hard candies is often helpful (especially mint candies).
- Ginger is an anti-nausea remedy; ginger ale may be helpful.
- Avoid smelling odors that cause nausea. Fresh air may make you feel better. It is sometimes helpful to leave the kitchen while food is being prepared or to have prepared food (from a deli, etc.) brought to you.
- Drink soups and broths to replace fluids if you're vomiting. Sports drinks are an excellent way to help replace fluids and electrolytes lost through vomiting.
- Check with your doctor about taking vitamin B-6 to help nausea. The usual dosage is 50-100 mg — do **not** exceed that dosage! Do not take extra vitamin and mineral supplements unless prescribed by your physician as high dosages can have harmful effects on the fetus(es).

You should be cautioned not to take medications for nausea and vomiting. Many anti-nausea medications contain antihistamines which have been shown to cause birth defects in animals. **You should check with your physician before taking any medications while pregnant.**

Heartburn

Some pregnant women develop heartburn. Like nausea and vomiting, there are some helpful measures you can try:

- Eat foods that are "easy on your stomach." Avoid greasy, fried, or spicy foods.
- Avoid foods that you've discovered give you heartburn.
- Eat small meals with frequent snacks between meals.
- Sip fluids throughout the day. Avoid drinking large volumes at one time.
- Eat a small amount of yogurt or drink a little milk.
- Try chewing papaya enzyme tablets, a pleasant tasting, natural digestive aid, before and after eating (available in health food stores). Check with your physician before eating these.
- Avoid smoking and drinking coffee, as both may irritate your stomach.
- Do not lie down immediately after eating. You may want to try a leisurely walk. You also may want to sleep and/or recline with your shoulders and head slightly elevated rather than lying down flat. Put books or a cinderblock under the head of the bed legs which will elevate the head of the bed a few inches (you will want to check with your physician before elevating the head of your bed since some pregnancy complications, such as incompetent cervix, may make this unwise).
- To relieve heartburn, try sitting cross-legged, rapidly raising and lowering your arms above your head, bringing the backs of your hands together over your head. Repeat a few times.

If your heartburn is unrelenting, your physician may prescribe a liquid antacid. Please don't take an antacid without consulting your physician (and don't take more than prescribed!). One note about taking antacids: some brands contain aspirin (Alka-Seltzer, Fizrin) and some contain large amounts of sodium (baking soda, Soda Mint, Eno, Fizrin, Rolaids, Alka-Seltzer). However, some brands are also high in calcium, which is often deficient in the diets of women pregnant with multiples. Check with your physician for his/her recommendation. Liquid antacids are usually more effective than tablets, because they do a better job of coating the esophageal lining. Be sure to ask your physician how much and how often over-the-counter antacids may be taken. These medications, taken in excess, can be very harmful.

Suggestions for Increasing Nutrition and Weight Gain

Many women find themselves in the situation of "falling behind" with their weight gain. This may happen in early pregnancy if you have nausea and vomiting and may make weight gain seem impossible. Some women even experience weight loss. What can you do if you are finding it hard to gain weight? The first thing is to realize how important it is to nutritionally gain weight. Next, make a project out of gaining weight. While rate of weight gain is important, "making up" for lost weight gain is better than not gaining the weight at a "proper rate." Following are some suggestions to help gain weight:

- Try making double-rich milk. Mix 1 cup instant powdered milk with 1 quart whole milk.

- Try concentrating protein. Mix a can of tuna with a cup of cottage cheese and eat it with bread and lettuce.

- Supplement meals with Ensure® (a liquid dietary supplement, Ross Laboratories). It is recommended that women drinking Ensure should drink only 2 (8 oz./day). Drinking more than that can lead to ingesting an excess of vitamin A.

- Get help from friends! When friends and relatives ask what they can do to help, let them know that you're having a hard time getting the food requirements you need. Ask them to bring you meals or portions of meals. Weight gain is a critical matter. People want to help in any way possible, so give them the opportunity!

Additional suggestions are:

- Grate cheese on casseroles, sauces, soups, scrambled eggs or vegetables.

- Choose dessert recipes which contain eggs.

- Add dry milk powder to recipes that call for milk such as soups, desserts or casseroles.
- Treat yourself to a high protein shake: 1 cup whole milk with 2 Tbs. of dry milk, 1/2 cup ice cream, 1/2 tsp. vanilla extract, 2 Tbs. of your favorite sauce – chocolate, strawberry, etc. Blend together at low speed about 10 seconds.
- Sprinkle sugar or honey into drinks or on cereal or fruit (15 calories/Tbs.).
- Spread peanut butter on fruit, crackers, bread or celery (80 calories/Tbs.).
- Drink fruit juices, especially fruit nectars or juice. (Women with gestational diabetes should not drink unlimited amounts of fruit juices.).
- Use mayonnaise for a dip for vegetables or crackers—also on sandwiches or in salads (100 calories/Tbs.).
- Avocados, oils, nuts, all will help you increase fat and calorie intake.
- Talk to your physician and see a registered dietitian! Don't fall into the trap of not getting help with your special nutritional needs.

Constipation

Constipation can plague some pregnant women, and could be a potential danger to someone trying to avoid preterm labor. Hormonal changes during pregnancy can cause the gastro-intestinal muscles to relax, causing constipation. The weight of the growing uterus can also cause this problem, particularly later in pregnancy. Constipation can cause uterine irritability which may progress to preterm labor. Straining to have a bowel movement may be associated with preterm rupture of the membranes (a very serious complication). If you experience constipation, it is important for you to resolve the problem as soon as possible.

If constipation becomes a problem for you, try the following:
- Eating high fiber foods such as fruits, vegetables, cereals and grains (i.e. prunes, raisins, figs, other dried fruit).
- Drinking plenty of fluids (2-3 quarts per/day). Hot or warm liquids in the morning and before meals may help.

- Check with your physician about taking a stool softener. Do **not** take any over-the-counter stool softeners or laxatives without checking with your physician first.

There are fiber sources for constipation that can be mixed with fluids such as Metamucil. Mixing Metamucil with *cold* orange juice is most palatable.

Adequate Rest Important

Another important thing to remember along with good nutrition is to get plenty of rest. A multiple pregnancy drains a woman's energy. Adequate rest will help you have an increased sense of well-being, appetite and ability to cope, better bodily functions (including digestion) and increased strength and energy. Allow for time to rest.

In Conclusion

Healthy eating is an important part of promoting a healthy pregnancy. Unlike other aspects of your pregnancy, you have control over what and how much you eat. Ask your physician about a comprehensive nutrition plan, or visit a registered dietitian and develop a program that is best for you. Work hard at eating right. It's important to do your best to help your babies be as healthy as possible.

The McColm children, Sandy, Utah

Endnotes

(1) Triplet Connection Medical Data Base. Information based on over 9,000 respondents to The Triplet Connection medical questionnaire who gave birth to triplets, quadruplets, or quintuplets.

(2) Abrams B, Newman V. Small-for-gestational age birth: maternal predictors and comparison with risk factors of spontaneous preterm delivery in the same cohort. Am J Obstet Gynecol 1991;164:785.

(3) Luke B, Minogue J, Abbey H, et al. The Association Between Maternal Weight Gain and the Birthweight of Twins. J Mat-Fet Med 1992;1:267.

(4) Luke B. Improving perinatal outcomes in multiple gestation through nutritional intervention. In: Care, Concern and Cure in Perinatal Medicine. Koppe JG et al (eds). 1992;477-485.

(5) Luke B. Maternal characteristics and prenatal nutrition. In: Multiple Pregnancy, Epidemiology, Gestation, & Perinatal Outcome. Louis KG, Papiernik E, Keith DM, Luke B (eds). The Parthenon Publishing Group. New York, London. 1995;304.

Multiple Pregnancy
Management and Birth

Your care during your multiple pregnancy will be more involved than a singleton pregnancy. The management of your pregnancy will likely require the following:

- Ultrasounds (including transvaginal ultrasounds)
- Tests (blood, urine, alpha-fetoprotein, amniocentesis, chorionic villus sampling, etc.)
- Biophysical Profiles
- Cesarean Delivery
- Planned Delivery

Ultrasounds

Ultrasounds are invaluable for any pregnancy. A woman pregnant with multiples may expect to have several routine ultrasounds throughout her pregnancy. They are especially important in a multiple pregnancy to determine a number of things such as the number of fetuses, the size of each fetus, the placement and number of placentas, and in monitoring growth and development of each fetus.

Transvaginal Ultrasounds

Studies show that pregnant women with long cervixes are not at risk for preterm labor and delivery, while women with short cervixes are. Transvaginal ultrasound is used to determine the length of the cervix. This cervical measurement can help the physician determine if the mother is at low or high risk for preterm labor and delivery at any time during pregnancy. Studies have shown transvaginal ultrasound to be an accurate indicator in singleton and twin pregnancies, and physicians are finding it to be helpful in higher-order multiple pregnancies as well. Cervical length measurement can help your physician determine what, if any, interventions may be necessary (strict bedrest at home or in the hospital, home uterine monitoring, drugs to prevent preterm labor, etc.).

Blood Tests

Blood tests provide your physician with information to help you have a healthier pregnancy. A blood test tells if you have anemia (iron-deficiency,) hepatitis B, HIV, syphilis, etc. All of these conditions will affect pregnancy management. A blood test is an important source of information.

Urine Tests

A urine test can detect urinary tract infections (UTIs,) and the presence of ketones and/or protein in the urine. A UTI requires treatment with antibiotics. Protein in the urine can be an indicator of pre-eclampsia or kidney disease. The presence of ketones in the urine can be an indicator of an inadequate amount of carbohydrates in the patient's diet, or an indicator that the patient is not eating an adquate amount of food (particularly protein).

Alpha-Fetoprotein (AFP) Test

The AFP test is an indicator of how much protein is being produced by the fetus and the fetal yolk sac. A low AFP can be an indicator of Down Syndrome or other genetic problems. An elevated AFP can be an indicator of spina bifida or neural tube defects. Because the AFP test measures a total level (not individual levels), it cannot tell what the AFP level is for each baby; it just gives a grand total. This test is fraught with problems in the case of multiple gestations. It often causes undue concern on the part of the parents and the physician, leading to additional unnecessary testing. For this reason, many physicians decline performing this test on multiple gestation pregnancies.

Amniocentesis

Amniocentesis is a procedure quite often used to determine if a baby has chromosomal abnormalities which are frequently age-related. It is usually offered to women 35 years of age and older, when the chances of Down Syndrome increase. This test will also detect neural tube defects. Though a normal amniocentesis test can rule out the presence of chromosomal defects, it does not test for all defects that can occur in the developing babies. This test does accurately determine the sex of your babies.

Using ultrasound to direct the safe placement, a thin needle is inserted through the abdomen into the uterus, where some of the amniotic fluid from each of the babies' amniotic sacs is collected for analysis. Test results are usually available within two weeks.

The procedure, in singleton pregnancies, is usually recommended between 15 – 20 weeks of pregnancy. Prior to 15 weeks complications of the procedure are higher, and after 20 weeks a therapeutic abortion is much more difficult should parents decide to abort due to test results. Late in pregnancy (33-38 weeks), amniocentesis is sometimes performed to determine whether a baby has adequate surfactant present to prevent respiratory problems.

In multiple pregnancies, there is some increase for potential problems due to amniocentesis, and many physicians feel that it is not worth the risks involved. In multiple pregnancies amniocentesis is often performed earlier than 15 weeks because if multi-fetal selective reduction is to be attempted it is usually done before this time. There is sometimes difficulty in obtaining fluid from each sac individually (particularly when there are three or more). In a small number of cases infection sets in, a sac is ruptured, or premature labor is instigated. In late pregnancy it is very difficult to get fluid from each individual sac, so sometimes determination of maturity is based on fluid from only one of the infants.

In singleton pregnancies, miscarriage due to amniocentesis occurs once in every 250-300 procedures. The loss is known to be higher in multiple gestation, but statistics are not available.

Chorionic Villus Sampling

Chorionic villus sampling (CVS) is similar to amniocentesis in that a needle is guided into the uterus either through the abdomen or vagina and cervix to collect chorionic villi (tiny projections taken from the chorion – a part of the placenta). Because this placental tissue contains babies' genetic material, it can be tested for many congenital conditions.

One of the advantages of CVS is that it can be performed much earlier in pregnancy, usually between the 10th and 12th week. Test results take about two weeks.

The disadvantage of the procedure is that CVS results are frequently abnormal in a multiple pregnancy, triggering fear and false alarm among expectant parents. The miscarriage loss in singleton pregnancies due to CVS is 1 in 100. The loss rate is higher in multiple gestation, but numbers are unavailable. The ability to adequately collect villi samplings from each individual baby in multiple gestations is difficult, particularly in the case of higher-order multiples. Many physicians feel that this test is too risky and the test results too unreliable for multiple pregnancies, especially when it's triplets or more.

Fetal Fibronectin (fFN) Testing

Fetal fibronectin (fFN) is the latest test approved by the FDA to help patients and physicians to predict risk of preterm delivery. Detecting fFN (a protein that is made by the amniotic membranes and the inner layer of the uterus) in the vaginal secretions between 24 and 34 weeks indicates an increased chance that delivery will occur prematurely. In patients either at risk for preterm delivery or patients in current preterm labor with the cervix dilated less than 3 cm, fFN testing can help to determine risk of delivery. The simple test (using a Q-tip to obtain a sample from the vagina), which takes between 6-36 hours (depending on the lab) can either reassure you that you will probably not deliver in the next two weeks, or alerts your physician to expect problems. Some physicians recommend fFN testing for multiple-birth pregnancies every two weeks between 24 and 32 weeks gestation. A positive test would prompt very intensive management including probable hospitalization and cortic steroids. Tocolytic drugs and antibiotics might also be started with a positive fFN test during these critical weeks. (See Appendix for article on Fetal Fibronectin Testing.)

Biophysical Profile Testing

Biophysical profile testing uses ultrasonography and fetal heart rate monitoring to assess certain biophysical variables in each developing fetus. In high-risk pregnancies, such as multiple births, biophysical profile testing may be indicated and is usually performed twice weekly during the last few weeks of pregnancy. If you are experiencing complications with your pregnancy (i.e. pregnancy induced hypertension, intrauterine growth restriction, etc.), biophysical profile testing may be recommended as early as 26 weeks or at the time that the complication appears. If no known complications are present, many physicians will begin biophysical profile testing by 32-34 weeks in order to keep a close watch on each of the developing babies.

Biophysical profile testing helps your physician to determine how *each* fetus is doing. The test is generally predictive for three to four days (that is to say, a biophysical profile test tells how each fetus is doing and is accurate for three to four days). After three to four days the test must be repeated to assess how the fetuses are doing for the next three to four days (at which point the test would be repeated). If the biophysical profile test indicates any problems with any of the fetuses, your physician will be able to evaluate and address the problem.

Perhaps the most important thing to remember about biophysical profile testing is that it can tell your physician if one or more of your fetuses is doing poorly. If your physician starts biophysical profile testing by 32-34 weeks or when complications arise and conducts it twice weekly, you and your physician will know the well being (or lack of well being) of your babies continuously. Some babies are lost because their fetal health begins to deteriorate, and no one knows it is happening. Biophysical profile testing is one way of determining the best time to deliver your babies and may help you have a better pregnancy outcome.

Planned Delivery

A new area of concern in higher-order multiple pregnancies is in carrying the pregnancy *too long*. With emphasis on avoiding preterm delivery and improving length of gestation (through nutrition, home uterine activity monitoring, bedrest, use of tocolytics, etc.), some higher-order multiple pregnancies may be delivered too late. A tremendous load is put on the placentas in higher-order multiple pregnancy. This may cause "preterm aging" or depletion of the placenta. The result of carrying the pregnancy too long may end with devastating consequences, such as the stillbirth of one or more babies. Most physicians recommend delivery of triplets by or before 37 weeks gestation. Again, twice weekly biophysical profile testing and diligent monitoring may help prevent unnecessary loss of babies in the last weeks of pregnancy. Indeed, there is controversy regarding the merit of letting a multiple pregnancy progress too far. Babies born at 36+ weeks gestation usually go home very soon after birth; oftentimes the babies go home with the mother.

Cesarean Delivery

As your pregnancy progresses, you will begin to think more about the arrival of your babies. Most physicians choose to deliver triplets by cesarean delivery. You will want to talk with your physician about cesarean delivery and read up on it in your pregnancy books. A vaginal delivery of triplets is not usually recommended, although there are dissenting opinions. The delivery time between the first and third babies can be delayed with vaginal delivery, causing fetal distress in the third baby born. Another problem with vaginal delivery is that the first (and/or second) baby(ies) may be born vaginally and the remaining one or two by cesarean (due to fetal complications or presentation or position of the second or third babies). It is indeed unfortunate when a woman successfully carries her babies to a healthy gestation only to have serious complications due to a vaginal delivery.

Birth

The birth of your multiples begins a new stage for you and your family. First, you're no longer going to be pregnant! For most mothers, the delivery brings tremendous relief — relief from anticipation, pregnancy worries, and most noticeably, physical relief. This is the long awaited time: the babies are arriving! Depending on the circumstances of the birth this may be a joyous time, but it may also be a stressful time if the babies are very preterm. Most multiples are delivered by cesarean section, but the details of your delivery may vary considerably depending on the gestational age of the babies and any other medical conditions or complications surrounding the birth.

Keep in mind that there will probably be a variety of health care professionals present during this time. You will recognize some of them (your physician, nurses, etc.), but there will be many additional people on the medical team such as an anesthesiologist, operating room nurses, neonatologists, and a wide variety of technicians (to draw blood, do ultrasounds, start I.V.s, etc.). This is typical during a multiple birth, and you shouldn't be alarmed.

The anesthesiologist should talk with you about the type of anesthesia he/she will use. If the delivery is rushed because of fetal distress or some other medical complication, you may have to have general anesthesia and you would not be awake for the birth of your babies. If the delivery is not rushed, you may have the option of having a regional block (spinal or epidural). With this type of anesthesia, you would be awake during the delivery. Talk with your physician ahead of time to make an appointment with the anesthesiologist to discuss your anesthesia options.

Cesarean Section Surgery

If you are worried about a cesarean delivery, ask your doctor for some written materials (or even a film to view) on the procedure itself. (See Appendix for film on triplet pregnancy/c-section birth.)

Briefly, a cesarean delivery is performed as follows:

First, epidural anesthesia is most commonly used. It involves injection of a local anesthetic into the epidural space surrounding the spinal cord. This numbs the abdomen by deadening the nerves leading to it. Keep in mind, the epidural itself is not a painful experience – it feels about like someone running a fingernail up your spine as it is inserted.

Once it has taken effect, your surgery will be pain-free.

A catheter is inserted into the bladder to empty it. The abdomen is then opened, usually through a horizontal incision made just above the pubic bone. This type of cut is used because it heals most effectively. The amniotic fluid is drained off by suction. The babies are delivered through an incision in the lower part of the uterus. The umbilical cords are cut, and the afterbirths removed. The manipulation of the uterus will not be painful, but may cause nausea and vomiting. The incisions in the uterus and abdomen are then sewn up. The mother is given an injection of ergonovine to cause the uterus to contract and to stop any bleeding. The entire surgical procedure, from incision to closure, is usually accomplished in about 30 minutes time.

The health of both you and your babies will be evaluated immediately after delivery. Once again, this can be a joyous time, but it may also be a stressful time if there are any serious problems with either yourself and/or one or more of your babies. It may be difficult to feel that this time is more than a "medical procedure," but it really is. Even if there are complications, these are your babies and this is their birth. Take pictures and have those you love around you. If you deliver by c-section with general anesthesia, it is especially important to have loved ones there — in the years to come they will be the ones to remember the actual birth. Once again, check into the rules at your hospital ahead of time so that you may make arrangements to have someone with you in the delivery room.

After the cesarean, you will be moved to a recovery area where you will be closely monitored until you are moved into your hospital room to recuperate. Pain medication will be administered as needed.

A c-section is major surgery and requires recuperation. The length of time to recuperate will vary depending on your circumstance. For instance, a mother who has been on total bedrest during the last months of pregnancy will take longer to recuperate from the c-section and the months of bedrest than a mother who is able to remain more active prior to delivery. This is a time to organize and accept help from those around you. A multiple birth is an exciting time, and many people want to share in that time by helping you and your family. Take advantage of this help!

Oftentimes, families feel like it's asking too much to accept help. Other times, it may be too tiring to have people around all the time. If this is the case, schedule people to come and help for a set time and then have some "family time" scheduled where just the immediate family is present. You may also want to consider having some "alone time," when you and your babies (or your spouse and your babies) can get to know each other. Tailor a schedule to fit your needs and remember that even in the best of circumstances this can be an exhausting time, so ACCEPT HELP FROM OTHERS!

It is wise to arrange for help early in the pregnancy. The early weeks of a multiple pregnancy are critical to the health and development of the entire pregnancy. The expectant mother will likely appreciate and *need* help early on, with the help continuing until after the delivery.

The rewards

Truly, the risks of higher-order multiple pregnancies are great. Taking every precaution available to ensure the healthy birth of your precious babies is advisable. Healthy babies are most often the result of committed parents who have educated themselves about their pregnancy, in combination with knowledgeable, concerned, committed physicians. If there is any advice we can give to expectant parents that transcends all else, it is that the sacrifice is worth it all in the end. There is no way to adequately describe the joy you will feel as you hold your precious babies in your arms!

With all the emphasis placed on being informed and becoming an active "partner" with your physician (rather than a passive patient), we want you to know that there's more — much more — to look forward to both during your pregnancy and afterwards. There's great joy in watching this miracle of life unfold.

Preterm Labor

Recognition, Treatment, Prevention

. . . I was three months pregnant when the ultrasound revealed triplets. We were excited, scared, and confused . . . I learned that bedrest, preterm labor, and terbutaline were part of my carrying triplets. At 25 weeks, I went into labor and started terbutaline . . . On and off, I would have contractions, and so I would drink 32 ounces of fluid, lay on my left side, and pray for them to stop . . . At 34 weeks I started having contractions while at the doctor's office. I was hospitalized. With a lot of prayer and the best doctors, I delivered by C-section at 37 weeks.

Triplet Connection Member Letter

As a woman pregnant with multiples, you will probably be hearing a lot about preterm labor. Preterm labor is the foremost threat to a multiple pregnancy. Left untreated, preterm labor can proceed to advanced cervical dilation and/or ruptured membranes, which may result in the delivery of infants who are too immature to survive or who may survive with major health complications. Your physician may use different drugs to stop preterm labor. The worrisome thing about preterm labor is that 70-80% of women who experience it do not seek help until the cervix has dilated and/or membranes have ruptured and labor has progressed to the point where nothing can be done. At this point, tocolytic drugs (drugs to stop labor) are ineffective. (1)

Detecting Preterm Labor

Why do women "delay" seeking care when experiencing preterm labor? Simply because they don't realize they are in preterm labor! Any woman pregnant with multiples is at risk for preterm labor. What does that mean to you in a practical sense? How do you know if you're experiencing preterm labor? The following signs *may* help you recognize preterm labor. However, you must realize that preterm labor is *often* undetected because the signs listed below are not present or are unrecognizable. Be sure to read the next section about Home Uterine Activity Monitoring. If you experience any of the following, please call your physician immediately:

- Uterine contractions (usually painless) – four or more contractions per hour.
- Back pain.
- Pelvic "heaviness."
- Increased vaginal discharge or foul odor of discharge.
- Change in color of vaginal discharge to pink or brown.
- Mild, painless cramping, intestinal or uterine.
- A feeling that things are "not right."

Your physician will typically watch very closely for any signs of preterm labor. Cervical examinations to check for cervical length, dilation and thinning will probably be performed routinely. If you even **suspect** that you are experiencing preterm labor, notify your physician immediately and **insist** on being seen or at least talking to your physician. **Do not take no for an answer, or be put off by office secretaries or nurses who tell you that what you are feeling is "normal."** Remember that preterm labor is an extremely common complication of multiple pregnancy. It is important to be monitored for contractions and to be examined by your physician if you at all suspect you are having preterm labor.

3

The D'Alfonso children, Cicero, New York

Endnotes

(1) Hall MH et al, The Importance of Preterm Birth in Elder MG et al (eds). Preterm Labor, Churchill Livingstone Inc. 1997;17.

Home Uterine Activity Monitoring

I went into the hospital for routine tests when I was at 26 weeks gestation. They put a monitor on me, and the nurse couldn't believe I hadn't been feeling my contractions. I was having contractions every 3 minutes. After three weeks of being in the hospital on every drug possible, I delivered my babies at 29 weeks.

Triplet Connection Member Letter

My doctor started me on home monitoring when I was 24 weeks along. I couldn't believe it! My first monitoring session told me I was having way too many contractions. I had to go in the hospital to be put on drugs, but I went back home. My babies were born at 34 weeks and 5 days.

Triplet Connection Member
Medical Questionnaire Response

I started using home monitoring when I was 25 weeks. It was inconvenient, but I was sure glad I used it. I was in the hospital with too many contractions for a week, but I went home on the terbutaline pump and didn't deliver until 35 weeks.

Triplet Connection Member Letter

3

As previously stated, the greatest risk you face with multiple pregnancy is preterm labor and delivery. Many factors may lead to a preterm delivery. Prevention of preterm (or very preterm) birth is essential to help ensure the birth of healthy babies. Home uterine activity monitoring (HUAM) may help you detect preterm labor in time to prevent preterm birth.

One of the most important problems encountered by women expecting higher-order multiples is their inability to feel preterm contractions. These imperceptible contractions may progress to preterm labor, and the pregnancy may be lost. Talk to your physician about HUAM to check for uterine contractions that you can't feel. Something as simple as HUAM may prove an invaluable help.

Many physicians use HUAM routinely and successfully with all their patients who are at high risk for preterm birth. Literally thousands of women who have used it in their multiple pregnancies have reported it to be tremendously beneficial in helping them detect their preterm contractions in time to seek intervention before it was too late to stop the progress of labor. The goal should be to start monitoring early enough to be of benefit, by at least 18-20 weeks for mothers expecting triplets or more. Unfortunately, some physicians wait for an indication from the expectant mother that she may be in preterm labor before starting HUAM, and it is sometimes too late by the time she is aware of contractions to stop them.

How does HUAM work? It consists of a monitor belt which is placed around the abdomen just below the naval. It is connected to a small recorder which collects and stores the information. This information is then sent by telephone to a center where it is assessed by perinatal nurses. The monitor (the same monitor which would be used in the hospital to check for contractions) has been found to be very accurate in picking up contractions which are not felt by the mother. A woman on HUAM can monitor at any time of the day or night if she feels worried that she may be experiencing too many contractions.

Some physicians do not feel that HUAM provides enough benefit to make it worth the expense and effort. In fact, there have been ongoing controversial reports issued by The American College of Obstetrics and Gynecology concerning the effectiveness of HUAM. On the other hand, the FDA has approved HUAM for preterm use for patients at the highest risk for preterm delivery. The feeling is often that patient education and close monitoring by the physician or daily contact by a nurse is adequate. If your physician has an education program and/or patient/nurse contact program set up, you will want to talk with him/her about it. Also discuss HUAM with him/her. Then you may make a decision about what type of care would best meet your situation.

Since HUAM may be instrumental in preventing preterm birth, there is a great potential for cost-saving for the patient, the patient's insurance company, and the hospital. The cost of every preterm birth is staggering, especially when that cost is multiplied by three for a triplet birth. The cost of HUAM is minimal when compared to the costs of preterm birth. If your insurance company is unwilling to cover the cost of HUAM, a call by your physician explaining the cost of preterm birth compared to the cost of HUAM may help the insurance company reconsider.

The decision about whether or not to use HUAM should be yours. If you are unsure after talking with your physician, you may want to obtain a second opinion from another perinatologist or obstetrician. It may be helpful to talk with a physician who uses HUAM and one who doesn't. Do not hesitate to get a second opinion about HUAM; it may save your pregnancy.

Self Monitoring for Contractions

Self-monitoring is a technique useful in *some women* to help them recognize preterm labor. However, studies have shown that very few women using self-monitoring techniques are able to adequately detect preterm contractions. This is how the self-monitoring technique is used:

1. Lie down with a pillow behind your back, leaning slightly to your left side.

2. Place your fingertips on your lower abdomen, feeling the entire lower abdominal area for firmness. If your uterus is relaxed, your fingertips will easily indent. If the uterus feels tight, you may be having a contraction. The more familiar you become with the feel of your abdomen, the more adept you'll become at feeling contractions.

3. If you feel a contraction, time it. You'll need to keep track of *how long* and *how far apart* contractions are. It's best to jot this information down.

4. If you're having four or more contractions per hour, call your physician.

Once you have notified your physician, drink 24 ounces of fluids to make sure you are adequately hydrated and lie down on your left side. Drinking fluids helps when you are having contractions which are due to dehydration. Lying on your left side helps to increase blood flow to the uterus. These measures may cause your contractions to subside. Some people have also found that dimming lights and making a conscious effort to relax can help to decrease the number and strength of contractions.

Some hints for self-monitoring:

- Do not lie flat on your back.
- A contraction causes the whole uterine area to tighten, not just one spot.
- Sometimes contractions can be felt starting at the lower abdomen and "spreading upward."
- Monitor several times daily.
- Remember, if you experience four or more contractions per hour or experience other indications of preterm labor, you need to call your physician. Keep in mind that preterm contractions are most often *painless*.
- Sometimes contractions are felt only as a dull, low backache; other times as a distinct aching or painful lower back. If your lower back hurts, you *should* be concerned!

Self-monitoring may help you determine if you're experiencing preterm labor. Remember, some contractions throughout the day are normal. The more you self-monitor, the more you will be aware of these "normal" contractions. Three or fewer contractions per hour may be considered normal; four or more per hour are cause for concern. If you suspect you are experiencing preterm labor, call your physician. Do not let anyone "pacify" or ignore your concerns. You should be checked! A false alarm may happen — even more than once or twice, but preterm labor is serious and needs to be given your full attention and respect!

Note: a good alternative to self monitoring would be to consider Home Uterine Activity Monitoring. See previous chapter for details.

3

The Foster family, Greeley, Colorado

Bedrest During Pregnancy

Bedrest during a higher-order multiple pregnancy is common. In fact, many physicians routinely prescribe bedrest at a certain point during a multiple pregnancy (often around 20 weeks gestation). This may be a challenging time for many women. It is difficult to rely on other people for so many things when you feel well enough to be doing them yourself. The importance of following your physician's advice cannot be stressed enough. Bedrest may save your pregnancy, but it may still be a difficult time.

The strictness of bedrest will vary depending on your situation. If your pregnancy is progressing without any complications, your physician may prescribe "moderate bedrest." In other words, you may just need to make sure you're spending a certain amount of time resting, oftentimes in a recliner. You may be allowed to be up enough to eat, shower and use the bathroom. You may even be allowed to be up and around for part of the day. A common recommendation is for you to get off your feet for at least two hours in the morning, afternoon and night, and to never be on your feet for more than one hour at a time. This type of bedrest is often recommended as a preventative measure during a higher-order multiple pregnancy.

At some point in your pregnancy you may be required to go on "strict" or "partial" bedrest. Your physician may order bedrest for complications such as:

- Bleeding and/or threatened miscarriage.
- Preterm labor or increase in intrauterine contractions (four or more per hour).
- Thinning of the cervix or cervical dilation.
- Preterm rupture of the membranes.
- Pregnancy induced hypertension and pre-eclampsia (toxemia).
- Incompetent cervix.
- Intrauterine growth restriction.
- A history of a prior preterm delivery.
- Preventative or precautionary measure in multiple pregnancy.
- Maternal exhaustion.
- Closer surveillance by your physician.

3

If your bedrest is prescribed because of a pregnancy complication, it will probably be more strict than that prescribed for an uncomplicated multiple pregnancy. Bedrest with complications may be especially stressful because of the worry involved. Some of the above complications will require medical intervention that may result in hospitalization. If your physician has prescribed bedrest, it is important for you to find out exactly what type of bedrest he/she means. Some suggested questions to ask your physician are:

- Am I allowed to be up from bed at all?
- Am I allowed to get up to shower and use the bathroom?
- Am I required to lay down at all times, or may I sit up? In a chair or recliner?
- Can I lay flat on my back or do I have to lay on my left side?
- If I'm allowed to sit up, for how long during each day?
- Can I rest on the couch or in a recliner?
- How should I handle keeping my doctor's appointments? (Should I be dropped off at the door and use a wheelchair, or am I allowed to walk from the car to the doctor's office? Should I lie down in the car and in the doctor's office, or may I sit?)

- Am I allowed to vacuum carpets? This may seem like an odd question, but the back-and-forth motion of vacuuming can cause enough physical strain that your physician may advise against it.
- May I do laundry?
- May I carry groceries?
- May I drive?

Just as the reason for bedrest may vary, the length of time that your physician prescribes bedrest may also vary depending on the reason for the prescribed bedrest. Your physician may or may not be able to tell you how long you'll remain on bedrest.

Some women may consider bedrest even if their physician does not prescribe it. Common sense tells you that you will have a better pregnancy when you are rested. At the least, you should feel better. The experience of thousands of women who have undergone multiple pregnancies would indicate that taking the pressure of a heavy, oversized uterus off the cervix may help avoid cervical changes which often lead to a variety of serious complications.

While on bedrest, there may be allowable exercises or muscle movements that may be recommended to help maintain muscle tone and circulation. Your physician may wish to work in conjunction with a physical therapist to prescribe therapy that is safe and appro-

The Greenwell family, Englewood, Ohio

priate for multiple pregnancy. Ask your physician about this. **Don't ever decide to exercise or even seek a physical therapist without your physician's recommendation!**

Coping With Bedrest

The importance of bedrest cannot be overemphasized. Due to discomfort, however, many mothers have found it nearly impossible to simply stay in bed. Recliners have been a great help to many, and several mothers have said that the rental of an electric hospital bed has been a fantastic help. The use of several pillows packed around overextended tummies is sometimes helpful. Full body pillows or foam wedges are also helpful to allow patients to lay on their side while still having something to recline against. Supportive wedges and pillows can be purchased at medical supply stores, discount stores, or specialty shops (such as linen shops). Most women have found sleeping to be very difficult during the last few weeks of pregnancy, but napping as often as possible during the day seems to help.

Immersion therapy, studied for its effect on amniotic fluid volume, may also help in coping with bedrest. Floating in a pool daily provides temporary relief from the musculo-skeletal burdens of a higher-order multiple pregnancy. Check with your physician before beginning any type of immersion therapy and never attempt to get in or out of the pool by yourself. Make sure the area around the pool is dry or at least has a skid-proof surface to help prevent slipping or falling.

Bedrest is most often anything but "restful." Rather, bedrest is often a *stressful* situation. It is not an easy task to remain in bed when the house is a mess, children need to be taken care of, laundry is piling up, and projects remain unfinished at work. Financial strain due to a loss in income may also take its toll. Interruption of normal marital intimacy may also be a source of frustration and tension between partners. Worries about the pregnancy may continually nag at both the father and the mother. Boredom quickly sets in, and days become very long.

How do you cope with bedrest? It may be easiest to look at bedrest as a chance to get caught up on many of the things you've been meaning to find the time to do. Things you might consider are: start a journal, design birth announcements, sew, knit, crochet, quilt, organize recipes, catch up with letters or thank-you notes, network by phone with family, friends, and other mothers and expectant mothers, do crossword puzzles, read, listen to tapes from your public library, watch television or videos, organize your files, do your Christmas, summer or school shopping by catalog, or complete photo albums. Take this unexpected free time as an opportunity to do some volunteer work. Many community organizations need people willing to make phone calls, address envelopes, or do whatever could be done while resting in bed. It is also a good time to work on projects or do homework with your school-age children, or even to consider taking a college correspondence course. If you are fortunate enough to have access to a personal computer, this could be a great time to finally discover its capabilities such as finances, home management, education, etc., or even to continue some part-time work utilizing your computer and telephone. Access to the Internet increases your options even further and can allow you to network with other women or support groups such as The Triplet Connection .

In addition to the above, you may want to take the time to learn more about your pregnancy and the birth of your babies. Get a chart showing fetal development and follow it as your pregnancy progresses. Read about child development and child care. You may also want to do some reading about preterm babies.

There are a few things to keep in mind while planning bedrest activities. Tocolytic drugs such as terbutaline may cause shaking hands that may make crafts and needlework tiring and frustrating. Magnesium sulfate (administered intravenously to stop preterm labor) causes drowsiness and may make reading and concentrating on tasks difficult or impossible. If you are prescribed drugs to prevent labor you may want to do activities that don't involve fine motor skills.

Late in pregnancy, particularly if there are complications, boredom may be replaced by an overwhelming desire to sleep. At this time you may want to be undisturbed. Well-meaning visitors may actually make bedrest more difficult and stressful if they are interrupting you at times when you would rather be sleeping or resting. Have your family help establish "visiting hours" if you choose to schedule time to rest. Some people find it convenient to schedule visitors at mealtimes. This helps to slow down and increase food consumption and reduces the strain of having to be "up" for visitors. Also, when the meal is concluded, there is a normal break which allows the visitors to excuse themselves or for you to excuse yourself due to tiredness or sleepiness. Phone calls can be particularly annoying and amazingly frequent. An answering machine may be a very worthwhile investment. Alternatively, do not hesitate to just disconnect your phone.

Bedrest While in the Hospital

Certain complications in higher-order multiple pregnancies may require bedrest in the hospital. Bedrest at home can be challenging. Bedrest in the hospital may be even more stressful, causing unique challenges. Hospital bedrest involves more medical intervention than home bedrest. The reason the physician is treating the mother in the hospital may be as simple as the need to use drugs that can only be given intravenously (i.e. magnesium sulfate to prevent preterm labor or intravenous antibiotics); however, other reasons may include complications such as advanced cervical changes, bleeding, ruptured membranes, or other complications such as pre-eclampsia. Your physician will typically order hospital bedrest only when he/she feels that the case cannot be adequately managed at home.

During hospital bedrest the mother and the babies will most likely be very closely monitored, and other medical procedures will be routinely done (vital signs, blood tests, ultrasounds, urine analyses, etc.). Often a physician may order hospital bedrest for preterm labor. The length of the hospital stay can vary significantly depending on the patient's response to tocolytics, and many other factors the physician must consider (gestational age, cervical dilation, patient history, complications, distance from home to the hospital, etc.). Some hospitals are offering boarding type arrangements in local apartments to women who do not need acute care but do require close proximity to the labor and delivery unit.

Hospital bedrest poses some unique challenges. The routine of the hospital becomes the mother's routine. This lack of control over when you eat, sleep, bathe, etc., can become very frustrating. Interruptions for blood pressure checks, fetal monitoring, and visits by physicians, nurses and friends can become tiring. Sharing a room with someone else may also be frustrating, but is often required to reduce the cost of the hospital stay.

Your comfort while in the hospital on bedrest is important, because discomfort creates stress and anxiety which works against the

3

overall good of serenity and rest. Do not hesitate to request a new hospital bed or mattress, specific visiting times (as much as possible), a discontinuation of monitoring of vital signs from 11 pm until 7 am unless they are essential, etc.

Hospital bedrest may be frustrating, but it may also be a comfort. If you have any questions or concerns, there are physicians and nurses available. Remember, you are in the right place to be treated immediately in case of an unexpected complication. If you have been put on hospital bedrest, there is a reason that you are there rather than bedresting at home. Your cooperation is very important. Once again, all the inconveniences you are experiencing are for the safe and healthy delivery of your babies and for your own health and well-being.

Bedrest may not have been what you expected or wanted when you discovered you were pregnant with multiples, but the sacrifice of a few weeks of bedrest may change the outcome of a complicated pregnancy and give you just what you wanted — healthy babies. A reminder — you're not alone. The Triplet Connection can offer you a network of others who are on, or have been on bedrest. There is a national organization, *Sidelines*, which offers support and resources to bedresting moms (see Appendix). And keep in mind, this is all to give your babies the best chance possible.

3

The Fall family, Spokane, Washington

The Garvey children, Libertyville, Illinois

Preventing Preterm Birth

What can you do to prevent preterm birth? You and your physician must both work to be aware of any condition that may cause preterm labor and delivery. The following section provides important considerations to help you prolong your pregnancy.

Early Diagnosis of Multiple Birth

Studies of women pregnant with multiples have shown that early diagnosis of a multiple pregnancy improves the outcome of the pregnancy. Ultrasound is typically used to diagnose multiple pregnancy.

Reduction of Work Duties and Leave From Employment

Many obstetricians and perinatologists recommend that women pregnant with multiples should take a leave of absence from their employment prior to 20 weeks gestation. For some, a much earlier leave is needed. You need to be aware that the type of work you do may affect your pregnancy. It is crucial that you talk with your physician on your first or second appointment about what type of work you should or shouldn't be doing. However, regardless of the original recommendation, you may find that you are unable to work for as long as planned. If you find you are not doing well due to the stress and strain of your pregnancy, talk to your physician about an earlier prescribed leave.

Researchers have compiled a list of work suggestions to help prolong pregnancy. Some of their suggestions are:

- **Prescribed work leave.** The basis for the effectiveness of work leave is twofold: (1) the patient's personal recognition that her work is tiring; and (2) the physician's willingness to act as the patient's advocate and to state that cessation of work is in her best interest and in the interest of her unborn child...the objective is to prevent preterm delivery, low birth weight, and the potential, long-term adverse sequelae [outcome] of both these conditions.

- **Modifying working conditions or hours.** Here, the physician can play an important role as intermediary between the patient and her employer to effect a change in work station; a reduction in the hours of unrelieved standing; or a cessation of heavy lifting, working in a cold, noisy, or wet area, or the manipulation of toxic substances. Oftentimes neither the patient nor her employer is aware of the potentially adverse implication of these conditions, and they will be receptive to temporary changes.

- **Decreasing household work and commuting efforts**. Poor quality of housing and a heavy burden of household activity was, [in this study] significantly related to preterm delivery. Moreover commuting to work using a number of transfer points also resulted in a higher rate of preterm delivery. Carrying groceries or small children, house painting, wallpaper hanging, and constant commuting may not be as innocuous [harmless] for pregnant women as previously thought.

- **Modifying activity**. Every patient should be advised to consider herself foremost during her pregnancy and to be attentive to the needs of her body. The patient should be told to stop all physical exertion when she perceives contractions, and, if possible, to lie down on her left side in a quiet, warm, calm environment. The patient should use a Home Uterine Activity Monitoring system if appropriate.

- **Continuing specific tasks.** Few guidelines exist that address specific tasks in terms of cutoff dates during pregnancy . . . the determination of whether a pregnant employee can or cannot do a particular job must be made on a case-by-case basis. (1)

The use of Home Uterine Activity Monitoring may be very useful in helping you and your physician determine when to modify activity and/or take a leave from work. An increase in uterine activity (detected by HUAM) can be instrumental in letting you know you're doing too much. The use of cervical measurement (determined by ultrasound) may also be helpful. See our chapter on Home Uterine Activity Monitoring (p.88), and our section on Transvaginal Ultrasounds (p.77) for more details.

In summary, working conditions that require standing, lifting and bending, or working around environmental hazards are suspect for causing preterm birth. You and your physician should determine what work you are able to do and when you should quit working during your multiple pregnancy. Even if your physician does not feel early work leave is necessary, if you are feeling overtired, overextended, or if you become uncomfortable working, it is probably best to push for an early leave. During such a pregnancy, it's important to take time to "gestate!" In other words, it takes making concessions in order to provide what is necessary for your well being and the well being of your babies. You'll have the rest of your life to return to work and to overextend yourself.

Endnotes

(1) Keith L, Luke B, et al. The Working Woman: Risks and Costs. Canadian Journal of Ob/Gyn & Women's Health Care. Vol 4: Num 6; 1992.

The Keefe children, Cumberland, Rhode Island

Managing Preterm Labor

Approximately 1 in 10 births in the United States are complicated by spontaneous preterm labor. (1) Among higher-multiple pregnancies, the incidence of preterm labor and delivery is significantly higher. Preterm labor is, in fact, the greatest threat to a higher-multiple pregnancy.

Management of preterm labor is critical. Once preterm labor is detected, there are a myriad of treatment options available. Your physician can discuss the options with you. It may be wise to have a discussion about preterm labor with your physician before it occurs. That discussion should include: signs of preterm labor, home uterine activity monitoring, procedures and options available if preterm labor is detected, and the use of tocolytics (drugs to stop preterm labor).

Your pregnancy may not be complicated by preterm labor, but you won't know whether or not it will be until your pregnancy reaches the point of delivery. It is important to know all that you can about preterm labor beforehand so that you can make informed decisions during your pregnancy.

If it is discovered that you are experiencing preterm labor, your physician may choose to treat it with tocolytic drugs. Some commonly used tocolytics are:

Ritrodrine and Terbutaline

Both are in a group of drugs called beta-sympathomimetic drugs. These drugs are most commonly used to stop preterm labor. Ritodrine was the first drug in the United States that was approved for treating preterm labor. Ritrodine and terbutaline work by causing the uterus to relax. A relaxed uterus will not contract and will not dilate the cervix. Studies have shown that these drugs do not have any harmful effects on the babies. The patient's heart rate will increase, since both of these drugs stimulate the heart. Side effects of the drugs could include nervousness, anxiety, tremors, nausea and vomiting, palpitations, chest pain, and fluid accumulation in the lungs (pulmonary edema).

When the above drugs are administered, the mother's heart rate, blood pressure, and uterine contractions will be monitored. The heart rates of the babies will also be monitored. Once the mother's heart rate reaches a certain level (typically 120-140 beats/minute), the optimal dosage has been reached. If preterm labor stops, the physician will wean the patient off the intravenous drug and typically will prescribe an oral dose. It is very important that the mother take the oral dose as prescribed, and especially important that it be taken on time. Delays in taking the medications may allow preterm labor to begin again. Usually, once preterm labor has subsided and the mother is taking the oral medications without labor beginning again, she may be sent home. Sometimes the physician will prescribe bedrest or partial bedrest at home.

Subcutaneous Terbutaline Pump Therapy

Many women experiencing preterm labor will be given terbutaline orally to stop contractions. However, some women taking terbutaline orally will experience "breakthrough" contractions or labor. That is to say, the oral terbutaline is not completely effective in stopping preterm labor. For these women, subcutaneous terbutaline pump therapy may be helpful.

Subcutaneous terbutaline pump therapy is an alternate way of taking terbutaline. A small plastic catheter or small needle is inserted just under the skin in the fatty layer or subcutaneous tissue of the thigh or abdomen. The catheter or needle is connected to tubing which attaches to a very small pump (about the size of a pocket calculator). The pump continually runs terbutaline through the needle into the patient and is capable of giving a bolus (a higher dose) if needed to control preterm labor. One word about the catheter or needle — it is very small and is placed just under the skin. Fortunately, the catheter or needle only needs to be changed about every three days and is much less painful to have inserted than to have an injection of terbutaline in the hip.

There are some advantages to using a terbutaline pump instead of taking terbutaline orally. First, it has been found to work in some mothers when oral terbutaline has failed or was not completely effective. Second, terbutaline pump therapy is effective at much lower dosages, which also substantially lowers the side effects of the drug. This lower dosage also allows the terbutaline to remain effective over a longer period of time. Third, terbutaline administered through a pump subcutaneously also acts more quickly to stop contractions than pills taken orally because it is absorbed into the patient's system more quickly.

Subcutaneous terbutaline pump therapy sometimes requires a few days stay in the hospital to determine the proper dosage for you and to teach you how to use the pump, though this is sometimes done in your doctor's office. Many women have prolonged their pregnancies significantly by using subcutaneous terbutaline pump therapy. You may want to discuss this therapy with your physician.

As with other therapies, some physicians feel that subcutaneous terbutaline therapy is not for everyone. Research has shown positive benefits (3), and countless members of the Triplet Connection have reported it has made a tremendous difference in outcome for them when they found themselves in preterm labor. Keep it in mind as an option for you if you're experiencing preterm labor and are taking tocolytics to control the labor, or if your doctor feels you must take labor inhibiting drugs for a prolonged period of time.

Magnesium Sulfate

Magnesium sulfate may be your physician's first drug of choice for preterm labor. The one drawback is that it can only be administered intravenously, which requires the mother to remain hospitalized while the drug is being given. Oftentimes the physician will use magnesium sulfate to stop preterm labor and then change over to a different tocolytic drug. Magnesium sulfate relaxes muscles, including the uterus. Due to this muscle relaxation, side effects include a "limp" feeling. It also has a sedative effect that causes drowsiness and "slower thinking." Other side effects include flushing and sweating and sometimes confusion and/or feelings of panic.

Magnesium sulfate can be given for a prolonged period (weeks to months). In some cases this may be necessary to prevent delivery of your babies. The side effects mentioned above are temporary, and most will disappear after 48-72 hours. If you need this drug in high doses, the side effects may seem unbearable at times. Work with the doctors and nurses to get through it; sometimes your only comfort will be the knowledge that it does not last forever. *More patients experiencing preterm labor deliver as a result of insufficient dosage of medication than from any other reason.* Your comfort must be balanced against preterm delivery of your babies. Your babies may not survive without this drug therapy.

Prostaglandin Inhibitors

Drugs such as indomethacin and naproxen sodium are prostaglandin inhibitors that may be used to stop preterm labor. Prostaglandin inhibitors easily cross the placenta, thus exposing the babies to these drugs. Some studies have shown these drugs to have a potential cardiovascular effect on the babies — specifically, the narrowing of the fetal ductus arteriosus (a blood vessel that connects the aorta and the pulmonary arteries), especially when administered after 34 weeks gestation. This narrowing has not been shown in studies to have any significant effect, but more studies need to be conducted. Many physicians limit their use of prostaglandin inhibitors to less than 34 weeks gestation. There are certain situations in which a physician will choose a prostaglandin inhibitor. Your physician can explain why he/she is using this type of drug.

Corticosteroids (Betamethasone)

The use of betamethasone helps speed the development of fetal lungs, reduces the effects of respiratory distress syndrome (RDS), and helps reduce the risk of bleeding in the infant's brain, or intraventricular hemmorhage (IVH). Betamethasone is a steroid given to women who are at risk of preterm delivery (preterm labor, ruptured membranes, pre-eclampsia, etc.). The drug needs to be administered 48 hours prior to delivery to get maximum effect on the baby's lung function.

Be aware that steroids can actually increase contractions, sometimes to the point of causing a patient to go into labor and deliver her babies as a result of the steroids. While the benefits of steroid use may outweigh the risk of increased contractions, close monitoring is essential during this vulnerable time.

3

The positive effect of the drug on the fetuses remains for about seven days. If a woman is threatening preterm delivery, the physician will prescribe the drug in the event that labor cannot be stopped and the babies are born early. If the mother does not deliver for seven days, the physicians will likely consider re-administering the drug if another episode of preterm labor occurs. Many physicians choose to give a mother betamethasone on a weekly basis if preterm delivery is considered likely. The mother or fetuses will not be harmed by betamethasone administration if the preterm labor stops and delivery does not occur. Some evidence also suggests that lung development is enhanced and IVH is decreased even if betamethasone is administered and preterm delivery occurs less than 24 hours after the drug is given. Even with very preterm delivery (less than 28 weeks gestation), the administration of betamethasone seems to help fetal outcome.

Long term effects of the use of betamethasone in preterm delivery have been conducted. Children have been followed for up to 12 years of age without showing any negative effects of the use of the drug.

FDA Approval of Drugs

Because many drug therapies which are currently and successfully being prescribed as tocolytics are not FDA approved at this time, an explanation of FDA approved drugs is in order.

Under the Federal Food, Drug, and Cosmetic (FD&C) Act, a drug approved for marketing may be labeled, promoted, and advertised by the manufacturer only for those uses for which the drug's safety and effectiveness have been established and which the FDA has approved. The FD&C Act does not, however, limit the manner in which a physician may use an approved drug. Once a product has been approved for marketing, a physician may prescribe it for uses or in treatment regimens or patient populations that are not included in approved labeling. Such "unapproved" or, more precisely, "off label" uses may be appropriate and rational in certain circumstances, and may, in fact, reflect approaches to drug therapy that have been extensively reported in medical literature.

As an example, Minoxidil is a drug which was originally approved by the FDA for the treatment of hypertension. It was also found to be a potent hair growing agent, and was safely prescribed by doctors for treatment of baldness for many years before it was finally FDA approved for hair loss treatment. Accepted medical practice often includes drug use that is not reflected in approved drug labeling. (2) It is common medical practice to use drugs which have been shown to be safe and effective, **even though that use is not reflected with FDA drug labeling**.

In time, many drugs which may have been approved for use in other countries where they are being used extensively and successfully as tocolytics and for many other uses, will be FDA approved. Meanwhile, use of a label-approved (but not FDA approved) drug may provide lifesaving benefits to you and your unborn babies.

In Conclusion

Preterm labor is very worrisome to the woman pregnant with multiples, her family, and her physician. Early detection is critical and will often save the pregnancy. Many women may feel unsure of themselves when they suspect preterm labor has begun. It cannot be stressed enough: if you even suspect that you're experiencing preterm labor, **call your physician**! Do not let anyone talk you out of doing this. Nurses or office staff may try to put you off when contacting your physician. Don't allow them to! It is better to go into the hospital or doctor's office and have it be a false alarm than to wait until it's too late! If your physician does not take you seriously, change physicians.

Preterm labor accounts for more than 75 percent of all infant deaths and complications. It is also important to realize that preterm labor may occur quite early in a multiple pregnancy, even as early as 18-20 weeks. Many doctors are not looking for labor this early. Too many pregnancies are delivered at this time, so be aware of your contractions whether you are using a Home Uterine Activity Monitor or self-palpating. Your pregnancy may be lost if you do not get treatment for preterm labor. But remember, preterm labor that is detected and treated early is usually a manageable condition. You can still have healthy babies, even if you have experienced early preterm labor. The important issue is to detect and treat preterm labor **before** a significant amount of cervical change has occurred.

3

The Amponin children, Mundelein, Illinois

Endnotes

(1) ACOG Technical Bulletin. Preterm Labor. Number 206, June 1995.

(2) Gabbe SG, Niebyl JR, Simpson JL (eds). Obstetrics. Normal and Problem Pregnancies. Churchill Livingstone. 1991. 2nd ed. p. 855.

(3) Lam et al. Clinical issues surrounding the use of terbutaline sulfate for preterm labor. Obstet Gynecol Survey 1998; 53(11):85-95.

The Firlotte family, Mentor, Ohio

Important Information

General Tips For All Pregnant Moms

Women pregnant with multiples sometimes don't realize that some seemingly "ordinary" activities may be harmful during pregnancy. The following tips may help you have a healthier and safer pregnancy:

- **Proper Seat Belt Positioning**. The American College of Obstetrics and Gynecology recommends wearing the shoulder strap of the seat belt and adjusting the lower part of the belt to fit *below* the woman's pregnant stomach. Improperly positioned seat belts (worn too high or too loose) can cause injury to both the mother and unborn babies. Non-use of seat belts is *never* recommended.

- **Exercise/Fitness Programs**. In an effort to have a healthy pregnancy many women use exercise videos or other fitness programs during pregnancy. While this may be safe for an uncomplicated singleton pregnancy, it is not recommended for a high-risk multiple pregnancy. Even exercise programs designed for use during pregnancy are not safe for a multiple pregnancy.

- **Positioning During Sleep and Rest**. A woman pregnant with multiples will have a healthier and more comfortable pregnancy if she sleeps and rests on her side, preferably her left side. While this is not as critical during the early weeks of pregnancy, it becomes important when the weight of the uterus, fetuses, and placentas become sufficient enough to compress the aortic artery. This vessel runs through the trunk of the body. Compression of this vessel inhibits the flow of blood throughout the body, which decreases oxygen flow to both the mother and the fetuses. Lying on the left side allows optimal blood flow to provide the circulation which in turn gives the babies more oxygen, nutrients, etc. Prop a pillow under your hip to position yourself on your side.

- **Overheating During Pregnancy**. A pregnant woman should be very careful to avoid overheating during pregnancy. Activities such as using spas, hot tubs, or saunas, excessive sun exposure, etc. can all cause overheating. This is especially critical during the early development of the fetuses (the first three months). Overheating of the mother can result in an increased rate of fetal abnormalities. It may also cause dehydration, which can contribute to preterm labor.

- **Sexual Intercourse**. Consult with your physician concerning sexual activity during your pregnancy. There are times during a high-risk, multiple pregnancy that sexual intercourse is not recommended.

- **Shortness of Breath**. Although rare, there are cases of maternal heart complications during and/or after multiple pregnancy. Shortness of breath, difficulty breathing and gurgling sounds when breathing are all signs that may indicate serious complications. Certainly, a very pregnant woman may feel like it's uncomfortable to breathe, but if your breathing is becoming difficult (i.e. cannot lie down because breathing becomes too difficult) either before or after delivery, **seek immediate medical help**.

> **At 22 + weeks, I felt a dull ache in my lower abdomen. I thought it would go away if I just rested for a while. I'll always be grateful that my mom was there and suggested I call the doctor. I soon found myself at the hospital in full labor, taking mag sulfate, and developed a severe case of pulmonary edema. The fluid in my lungs made it almost impossible to breathe. I started seeing stars and felt**

like I was going to pass out. During the night I told the nurse it was hard to breathe and that I could hear a gurgling in my chest. She just smiled and said, "We can't do anything until the doctors make rounds in the morning." That was the scariest night of my life, and I found out later that I could have died. It's important to ask more questions than I did, and not to assume you're in good hands just because you're in the hospital.

—SM in Kentucky (1)

[Note: In extreme cases such as described above, do not hesitate to call your physician at home, even if you're in the hospital! Chest gurgling is not normal in any textbook of medicine, in men or women, regardless of whether they are pregnant or not.]

The Bryant family, Madison Heights, Virginia

Endnotes

(1) *The Triplet Connection Newsletter*, 1996:Vol. 13, No. 4, p. 31.

Possible Complications
of Pregnancy

4

Discovering you're pregnant with triplets or more is an exciting time. You will probably experience all types of emotions ranging from feeling excited to feeling overwhelmed. Once things have settled down, it is important that you take the time necessary to learn all you can about your multiple pregnancy.

Your multiple pregnancy is a high-risk pregnancy. Do not let anyone try to convince you otherwise. You will have a greater chance of developing complications during your pregnancy than if you were pregnant with just one or even two babies. If you do develop complications, it is important to know at least a little about each complication so that you may make decisions that are right for you and your family. Women who have taken the opportunity to educate themselves about their pregnancies will learn to watch for different "warning signs" indicating possible complications. It is also important for you to have close contact with your physician and his/her health care team. It is very important for you to establish good rapport with the physicians and nurses involved with your care. This care and rapport can be invaluable in establishing the best plan of care and treatment for your multiple pregnancy.

A multiple pregnancy requires more care and closer management than a singleton pregnancy because the success of your pregnancy depends on the early detection of a wider variety of possible complications. The goal of this "careful management" is simply to prolong gestation and well-being of the mother and babies. Management of a multiple pregnancy typically includes:

- Trying to determine the number of fetuses and their placental/ membrane relationships very early in the pregnancy.
- Prevention of preterm labor and birth.
- Close monitoring of fetal growth and well-being.
- Making sure that there is adequate medical care for the possible birth of preterm babies.
- Close monitoring of the health of the mother.

This is how "more care" and "closer management" is likely to be translated into your daily life:

- Your nutritional requirements will dramatically increase.
- Your physician may recommend a leave of absence from full-time employment prior to 24 weeks gestation.
- You will see your obstetrician or perinatologist more frequently and require more ultrasound evaluations than your friends carrying singleton pregnancies.
- You may experience preterm labor which may require medication to control.
- Your physician may recommend bedrest at some point in your pregnancy.
- You should be on the alert for any signs or symptoms of maternal health complications.

The biggest challenge that you and your physician face during your pregnancy is to "keep on top of things." Studies have shown that multiple pregnancies are most successful when your doctor discovers early on that you are carrying more than one baby. Once this is discovered, your physician will be doing a number of things which **may** include:

- Close monitoring of your pregnancy (for both fetal and maternal well-being).
- Home uterine activity monitoring.
- Early hospitalization (if needed).
- Aggressive therapy with tocolytic drugs (drugs to stop labor), if needed.
- Delivery by cesarean section.
- The presence of neonatologists (physicians specializing in the care of newborns) at the birth.

Sometimes the details of the care and management of your pregnancy may seem overwhelming. For the next several months, you and your physician will concern yourselves not only with the complications associated with multiple pregnancies, but also with the "ordinary" types of things that may complicate any pregnancy. That may mean a lot of worrying. The information in this chapter will help you understand some potential complications, and, hopefully, ease your worrying. As you read this information, remember that this chapter provides information about a wide variety of complications that you may possibly face during your pregnancy. Keep in mind, you won't face them all, and you may not face any of them. Being aware of possible complications and their symptoms, however, can sometimes be lifesaving.

Bleeding

Any bleeding during your pregnancy is frightening, but bleeding can occur for many different reasons. Early first trimester bleeding may be caused by implantation of the fertilized egg(s). Spotting can occur when the egg implants by burrowing into the uterine lining. This is normal, and there is usually no cause for concern. The cervix also bleeds easily, and bleeding from the cervix itself is usually not a cause for alarm. Cervical exams or sexual intercourse may also cause cervical bleeding.

Bleeding during the first trimester may also be a sign that a miscarriage is about to occur. This is termed a "threatened miscarriage" or a "threatened abortion." This type of bleeding sometimes "settles down," but may also proceed to a miscarriage. Miscarriages happen for a variety of reasons. Some miscarriages occur simply because the egg is non-viable (not living), or because there were serious problems with the development of the fertilized egg. If this is the case, nature will take its course and the pregnancy will miscarry. Your physician will ask questions and examine you to determine if you are "at risk" to miscarry. If you are at risk, your physician will talk with you in detail about his/her plan for following your pregnancy.

Bleeding or spotting during your pregnancy should be immediately reported to your physician. Typically, when a woman is spotting or bleeding during the first trimester the physician will have the patient lie down and rest. You'll often be gently told to "relax." Although it's frustrating, during the first trimester there isn't much to be done except to rest and hope that the bleeding stops. Many times, bleeding will occur and stop without your knowing what caused it.

Bleeding during the third trimester is an indicator of trouble and should be reported to your physician **immediately**. Some conditions that cause bleeding during the third trimester can be life-threatening to both you and your babies. Two life-threatening conditions are **placenta previa** and **abruptio placenta**. Placenta previa occurs when the placenta is located lower than normal, or very near the cervix. In some cases, the placenta may cover all or part of the cervix. Abruptio placenta occurs when the placenta prematurely separates from the uterine wall prior to delivery of the babies. Both conditions may lead to excessive and occasionally life-threatening bleeding. Once again, **immediately** report any third trimester bleeding to your physician.

Premature Rupture of the Membranes

Premature rupture of the membranes (PROM) is defined as the rupture of membranes before the onset of true labor. There are many causes of PROM such as:

- Incompetent cervix
- Vaginal bacterial infections
- Trauma
- Multiple pregnancy

The incidence of PROM during the second trimester of a singleton pregnancy is relatively rare, only 0.52%. The incidence during a twin pregnancy (again, second trimester PROM) is also low, about 1.37%. The incidence of PROM during the second trimester for a woman carrying triplets jumps to an alarming 15%. The cause of this increase is unknown, however,

". . . important factors include the rapid growth of the uterus, which causes preterm stretching and thinning of the cervix, as well as increased intrauterine pressure secondary to uterine contractions not perceived by the mother." (1)

A big concern with PROM is that infection may set in and force delivery of very preterm babies. The treatment for PROM depends upon how far along you are in your pregnancy. If it can be established that the babies are mature enough to be delivered, there may be no attempt to prolong the pregnancy. But in preterm pregnancies (especially those less than 34 weeks), the treatment of PROM may become more involved.

The traditional treatment of second trimester PROM has been either to induce labor or to wait for spontaneous labor and delivery. Delivery at this time (especially before 24 weeks) obviously would lead to a high rate of fetal complications and death.

There are also cases of PROM in which the membrane reseals, amniotic fluid re-accumulates, and labor does not progress to a point that forces delivery of any of the babies. In this case, the pregnancy may continue with all babies surviving.

Some physicians take the view that PROM signals the end of the pregnancy, and are not motivated to aggressively treat the complication. If you have membrane rupture and your physician sends you home to "wait and see," you should be checking with another physician for a second (or third) opinion. Sometimes this "wait and see" attitude is a result of money saving measures by clinics and hospitals (it's less expensive to lose a high-risk pregnancy early on than to try to save it with aggressive intervention). Be aware that many women, having experienced PROM as early as 19 weeks or before still go on to deliver healthy, near-term multiple babies after weeks or months of aggressive intervention.

Prevention of second trimester PROM is a much better alternative than the above scenario. With triplet pregnancies, some physicians are beginning to place elective cerclages in their patients early in the pregnancy. However, a preventative cerclage still remains very controversial as it sometimes causes serious complications or pregnancy loss (such as infection or accidental rupture of membranes). An alternative to elective cerclage placement is periodic ultrasound examinations of the cervix utilizing a vaginal transducer. These exams may detect cervical

4

changes, allowing for treatment before the mother progresses to PROM. Since second trimester PROM is such a threat in triplet pregnancies, it is important that the mother is carefully observed for cervical changes between 16 and 28 weeks gestation.

If you experience PROM, talk with your physician about the treatment options. Delivering all babies may certainly not be in your best interest. You may have success using some of the other treatment options. *The Triplet Connection has a packet of information available regarding PROM which can be mailed or FAXed immediately if you find yourself in this situation.*

> **A mother, whose water broke at 19 weeks of pregnancy (and continued to leak amniotic fluid for the remainder of her pregnancy), delivered healthy babies at 32 weeks. She was put on antibiotics, watched carefully, and participated in strict bedrest until delivery.**
>
> **A Triplet Connection Member (2)**

The Groff family, Jefferson, Maryland

... At 16 weeks gestation ... I noticed that I had started to bleed. The doctors felt I had placental abruption. I was immediately placed on complete bedrest ... Four weeks later at 2:00 a.m. our worst fears were realized when I woke up in a pool of warm water... We rushed to the hospital, both shaking and in tears. We learned that Brandy's amniotic sac had ruptured. We were terrified, feeling we were about to lose our long-awaited babies.

We were informed that I would likely go into labor within 48 to 72 hours. The doctors told us that after the delivery of Brandy, they would make every effort to keep Michael and Cody from being born. The emotional pain was incredible. We were hopelessly in love with each one of our precious babies.

The following morning I woke to another pool of water — the rest of Brandy's amniotic fluid ... An ultrasound was performed every week, and every day that Brandy was still living was a miracle. Her membrane never did seal. Every morning I awoke to a pool of water, and her sac continued to leak during the day. Her amniotic sac was hopelessly dry.

Winter turned to spring. Christmas, Valentine's Day, my birthday, St. Patrick's Day, and Easter all passed, and I was still in the hospital ... At 32 weeks I went into labor. Brandy was under so much stress that it was too dangerous to try to stop it so we didn't ... the babies arrived by c-section. Our babies were all incredibly healthy, including Brandy! We were able to bring them home when they were between two and three weeks old.

—DL in Washington (3)

Delayed Interval Deliveries

Within the past few years some physicians are having increasing success in delaying the complete delivery of a twin (or higher-order multiple) pregnancy. Often, intra-amniotic infection associated with PROM or just precipitous preterm labor that cannot safely be stopped leads to the birth of a very premature infant. If the remaining fetus(es) have their own placenta(s) and it is known that they are otherwise well and show no evidence of infection, it may be possible to delay their delivery by days or even sometimes many weeks, allowing for greater maturity in utero.

There are many treatment strategies to accomplish this, but the treatment in the largest reported series of patients generally included the use of aggressive tocolysis, antibiotics, and cerclage procedures. These are very high-risk situations which require close surveillance both as an in-patient and eventually as an out-patient by physicians who have interest and experience in delayed interval deliveries. It is very important to know when it is no longer advisable to continue the pregnancy [often when there is evidence of infection in the remaining fetus(es)]. It is also important to know which pregnancies are good candidates in the first place, so that these delayed deliveries can be safe for the mother and remaining fetus(es) and there is a reasonable likelihood of success. *If you find yourself in such a situation, we have a number of doctors who have successfully managed cases and who are happy to share their experiences with you and your physician. We have a packet available for those who experience PROM or delayed-interval delivery.*

The Blackburn children, Laguna Hills, California

A mother whose first baby was delivered at 27 weeks held off delivery of her subsequent two infants until 34 weeks. Needless to say, there were tremendous challenges in the seven weeks she continued her pregnancy, but her persistence (and that of her husband), combined with excellent medical care . . . allowed her two remaining babies to be born healthy. (4)

Libby was confident that she'd make it to 34 weeks with her triplet pregnancy and have 5 pound babies. She was eating right and using home monitoring . . . Everything seemed perfect.

Later that day, however, Libby found herself in the hospital in preterm labor; she was dilated 3 centimeters with one baby's head very low. Her doctor finally got the contractions stopped, but not before Rachel Anne was born at 2 pounds, 2 ounces. In most cases, the obstetrician would have gone ahead and delivered the remaining babies, but [the doctor] had had a similar case about five years previous in which the woman went into labor and lost all of her babies. This time he wanted to save as many babies as he could. He chose to deliver one and then see if the others would stay put.

The day after Rachel's birth, Libby's cervix had closed to one centimeter, so she did not have a cerclage. Libby remained on bedrest in the hospital, [the doctor] monitored her condition and that of the two unborn babies.

Like many preterm babies, Rachel suffered from respiratory distress syndrome . . . On August 9, eleven days after Rachel's birth, Libby developed a fever, and one of the two babies had a cord wrapped around her neck. Libby had an emergency C-section. Blair Elizabeth and Emily Dana came into the world weighing 2-6+ and 2-8+ respectively . . While Blair and Emily stayed for 66 days in the ICU, Rachel stayed 84 days.

continued next page

Today, Rachel, Blair, and Emily are getting stronger and bigger . . . Libby and her husband are grateful to their obstetrician for the way he chose to manage the deliveries, and they feel lucky to have all three girls healthy and happy.

—LS in Maryland (5)

Pregnancy-Induced Hypertension and Eclampsia (Toxemia)

Pregnancy-induced hypertension (PIH) is a condition of high blood pressure that occurs only in pregnancy. The cause of PIH is unknown, although in some cases it seems to "run in families." PIH often requires that the mother be hospitalized. However, mild cases may be followed without hospitalization but with frequent visits to the physician. The problem with PIH is that it may lead to eclampsia. Eclampsia is a serious condition wherein the patient may have convulsions, go into a coma, or both. Eclampsia is a treatable condition. Left untreated it may lead to death of the mother, fetus, or both. The signs of PIH are:

- Elevated blood pressure
- Protein in the urine (diagnosed by testing a urine sample)
- Edema (generalized fluid retention and swelling)

Once PIH is diagnosed, physicians aggressively treat the mother to avoid the progression to eclampsia. If the babies are mature enough to be delivered, the physician may deliver the babies. If the babies are preterm and not ready for delivery, the mother will usually be admitted to the hospital and may be given the drug magnesium sulfate to prevent seizures. This drug is given through an IV or (rarely) by injection. Blood tests, urine tests, and daily weight checks are routine for the hospitalized mother with PIH. After the mother's blood pressure has lowered and she is otherwise stable, she may possibly be sent home from the hospital with a routine of daily blood pressure monitoring.

There is some evidence that one low-dose aspirin (81 mg), or baby aspirin a day may prevent or affect pre-eclampsia. Some physicians have found that mothers who take one low-dose aspirin a day beginning at 14-16 weeks until delivery have a lower incidence of pre-eclampsia, and if it does develop it appears later in pregnancy and is milder. For an explanation of aspirin therapy to prevent pre-eclampsia and toxemia, see Appendix article.

Incompetent Cervix

An incompetent cervix can be cause for loss of pregnancy during the second trimester. It's difficult for your physician to determine if incompetent cervix is a risk in your pregnancy. Here's why: Incompetent cervix is defined as the painless opening and thinning of the cervix. This dilation and thinning of the cervix leads to bulging and rupture of the membranes, which may lead to delivery. There are different causes for incompetent cervix, but no test is available to determine who is at risk for it or even to determine if the cervical dilation and thinning you may be experiencing is actually incompetent cervix. Dilation and thinning of the cervix may be normal late in your pregnancy, but is usually abnormal prior to 30 weeks. It's difficult for a physician to tell the difference between incompetent cervix and normal cervical thinning and dilation.

So, how does a physician decide if you have incompetent cervix? If your physician suspects that you may have an incompetent cervix he/she will probably do frequent cervical exams during the second trimester to watch for cervical changes. Ultrasound is also useful. If your physician determines that you do have an incompetent cervix, she/he will talk with you about treatment which may include bedrest and/or cerclage placement (a stitch around the neck of the cervix to help keep it closed). The following conditions may cause incompetent cervix:

- DES exposure
- Family history
- Previous pregnancies with incompetent cervix
- Previous cervical trauma (previous obstetrical or gynecological procedures, cone biopsy, obstetric lacerations, second trimester abortions)
- Previous, painless second-trimester pregnancy loss

A history of any of the above conditions are causes to signal your physician to watch for incompetent cervix. These conditions alert your physician, but do NOT necessarily mean that you have an incompetent cervix.

Intrauterine Growth Restriction

Intrauterine growth restriction (IUGR) occurs when fetal growth is less than what would be expected for the gestational age of the fetus. Simply, the baby is small for its gestational age. In the case of multiples, IUGR can occur when one baby is not in an ideal position to receive the proper nutrition. Due to overcrowding or just the position of the fetus, he/she may begin to lag behind in growth. IUGR may also occur for a variety of reasons. Some causes are serious, including chromosomal abnormalities, inherited genetic disorder, or infections. Other causes of IUGR may stem from health problems that the mother has (i.e. high blood pressure, ongoing kidney disease, etc.). The nutrition and lifestyle of the mother may also cause IUGR. Poor nutrition, smoking, and alcohol consumption during pregnancy are all causes of IUGR.

Once IUGR has been diagnosed there are some simple, yet effective measures that may be taken to help the fetuses:

• Good nutrition

• Stopping smoking and/or consumption of alcohol

• Increasing uterine blood flow to the fetuses

• Bedrest (to allow the mother time to lie on her left side to increase blood flow to the fetuses).

If one or more of the fetuses has IUGR because of disease, structural abnormalities, chromosomal abnormalities, or a genetic disorder, etc., your physician will discuss your treatment options. If, on the other hand, a baby is falling behind due to inability to receive proper nourishment, the doctor will want to watch the progress of the pregnancy carefully. In some cases, it may become necessary to deliver all the babies earlier than planned in order to save the baby who is falling behind.

Preterm Labor or Increase in Uterine Contractions

As a woman pregnant with multiples, you should be hearing a lot about preterm labor. Preterm labor is probably the greatest threat to your multiple pregnancy. Left untreated, preterm labor may proceed to advanced cervical dilation and/or ruptured membranes which may result in the delivery of infants who are too immature to survive or who may survive with major health complications. Your physician may use different drugs to stop preterm labor. The worrisome thing about preterm labor is that 70-80% of women who have preterm labor do not seek help until the membranes have ruptured and/or the cervix has dilated to the point where nothing can be done. At this point, tocolytic drugs (drugs to stop labor) are ineffective. (6) For a complete discussion of preterm labor, see the chapter, "Preterm Labor, Recognition, Treatment, Prevention." Because preterm labor is probably the greatest threat to your pregnancy, please take time to read that chapter!

Gestational Diabetes

4

Gestational diabetes is so named because it occurs in pregnant women who have had no previous signs of diabetes. Gestational diabetes should not be confused with Type I Diabetes which is also known as insulin-dependent diabetes. Gestational diabetes occurs in about 3-5% of pregnant women (statistics are not available for gestational diabetes among higher-order multiple pregnancies). (7)

Gestational diabetes is caused when the action of insulin is decreased by the presence of pregnancy hormones. A pregnant woman who has gestational diabetes still produces enough insulin, but the pregnancy hormones that her body produces interfere with the action of insulin. Gestational diabetes is controlled through diet and exercise, though occasionally insulin may be required during pregnancy to achieve adequate control.

Who is at risk for developing gestational diabetes? The following factors put you at risk:

- Multiple pregnancy
- Family history of diabetes
- Previous unexplained stillbirth
- Previous birth of a large (over 9 lbs.) infant
- Previous birth of an infant with multiple birth defects
- Maternal obesity
- Maternal age over 25
- Maternal hypertension

Even if you do not fall into any of the high-risk categories, it is recommended that all pregnant women be screened for gestational diabetes. Screening consists of a glucose challenge test. Typically a pregnant woman drinks a glucose solution and her plasma glucose is tested after a certain time (usually after 1 hour). If her plasma-glucose level is high, more testing is done (a glucose tolerance test) to diagnose gestational diabetes.

Once gestational diabetes is diagnosed, an individualized program should be tailored to help the patient control her blood sugar levels. This is done through careful diet and exercise. It is especially important for a woman pregnant with multiples (and diagnosed with gestational diabetes) to have a program set up to control her blood sugar AND still provide adequate nutrition for a multiple pregnancy. Exercise to help control gestational diabetes is also a concern with a woman pregnant with multiples and should not be undertaken unless recommended by the patient's physician. A registered dietitian would be qualified to develop an individualized program to nutritionally control gestational diabetes. The majority of gestational diabetic women can control their blood sugar by diet alone. (8)

Gestational diabetes is not associated with birth defects (Type I diabetes is associated with birth defects). However, it may cause larger than normal babies due to the high level of sugar in the fetal blood. Complications from gestational diabetes are manageable at the birth, though the infant's hospital stay may be longer because of associated complications.

Gestational diabetes is a complication of pregnancy that requires close care and monitoring, patient education, and strict cooperation. It is very important for you, your physician, and your registered dietitian to work as a team to help you have the healthiest pregnancy possible.

Itching During Pregnancy

Many pregnant women will experience itching during their pregnancy. This may seem like a minor complaint, but it can be severe, unrelenting itching that lasts for many weeks. Many patients are told by their physicians that hormones are the cause of their misery, and that nothing can be done to help.

Thankfully, many mothers are finding relief! So, if you're severely itching (more than merely as the result of stretching of skin), you might ask your physician to investigate the following possible causes:

Pruritic Urticarial Papules and Plaques of Pregnancy (PUPPS)

This condition is also manifested by intense itching, and very pronounced, characteristic skin eruptions. PUPPS usually begins on the abdomen, and spreads to involve the thighs, buttocks, and occasionally the arms. Often halos of blanching (paling of the skin) surround the eruptions. Most patients have hundreds of lesions, which usually resolve within 2 to 4 days with frequent applications of prescription triamcinolone acetonide cream. At times, oral prednisone is necessary to control the severe itching. Some patients have been prescribed antihistamines. This condition is usually treated by a dermatologist working with your physician.

Cholestasis (Pruritus) of Pregnancy

This is a relatively common condition, apparently caused by hormonal effects on the bile transport process. Severe itching is the most dominant and disturbing feature of cholestasis of pregnancy, and if untreated may involve the trunk and extremities, including the palms of the hands and soles of the feet. Insomnia, fatigue, and mental disturbance often accompany the condition. Mild jaundice may follow in one to two weeks, although it may not occur at all, or may follow many weeks later. In those with jaundice the urine becomes darker, and light colored stools are often reported. Though the condition is benign and disappears after delivery, it may recur with subsequent pregnancies or when taking birth control pills.

A prescription of oral cholestyramine may relieve the itching (by lowering serum bile acid levels — the source of itching). One should note that this medication can interfere with vitamin K absorption (increasing chances of hemorrhage), so vitamin K therapy would likely be instigated. Vitamins A, D, and K may also need to be supplemented during this drug therapy. Symptomatic treatment may suffice in milder cases and corticosteroids may be required in more severe cases.

HELLP Syndrome and AFLP

Mothers should be aware that through The Triplet Connection we have been in contact with a good number of women who, after having had cholestasis of pregnancy, developed a very serious liver-related condition known as HELLP Syndrome (hemolysis, elevated liver enzymes, and low platelet count). This condition is not known to be medically related to cholestasis of pregnancy, yet we are hearing from many women whose HELLP Syndrome was preceded by severe, unrelenting itching (often diagnosed as cholestasis of pregnancy). Additionally, in checking with our members who have reported developing HELLP Syndrome, many reported having experienced severe, unrelenting itching just prior to developing HELLP Syndrome. For this reason, we believe it is advisable to ask your physician to closely monitor liver enzyme levels (determined through simple blood tests) during and in the weeks following the onset of cholesatasis of pregnancy. By requesting to be monitored after developing such itching (though many of their physicians did not feel it necessary), several of our members were able to be treated very early for HELLP Syndrome. This is a condition which can be fatal to all infants and is extraordinarily dangerous for the expectant mothers. Acute fatty liver of pregnancy (AFLP), also a life-threatening complication, is often associated with intense itching. Many of the warning symptoms of HELLP Syndrome and AFLP are closely related to those of cholestasis of pregnancy because they also affect the liver.

AFLP and HELLP can also be life-threatening to infants whose mothers developed these conditions, but who survived birth. Modified diets may be life-saving to these infants (see article in Appendix).

As you can see from the above discussion, there may be several causes for severe itching during pregnancy. You might want to ask your doctor to investigate things a bit further if you're itching for an answer!

Group B Strep Infection

In a nutshell, Group B Streptococcus (GBS) is a vaginal infection, carried by the mother, that can infect newborns. The infection may be transmitted from the mother to the babies when premature rupture of membranes (PROM) occurs, or when babies pass through the birth canal in a vaginal birth. It is a deadly infection that can cause serious handicaps and death. Screening is available to determine if you are a GBS carrier.

Most people have heard of "strep throat." Strep throat is caused by an organism named Group A Streptococcus. Group B Streptococcus is another organism which may cause serious complications for your newborns. Group A Strep and Group B Strep are two different organisms and **should not be confused**. Our discussion pertains only to Group B Streptococcus.

GBS is carried by 15%-35% of women, regardless of race or socioeconomic status. Women who have been screened and carry a large amount of GBS are said to be "colonized." Colonized women typically do not have any symptoms and are unaware that they are carrying GBS until they are screened and test positive or have a newborn infected with GBS.

Why do physicians screen for GBS? GBS causes infections and meningitis (infection of spinal fluid and the brain) in newborns. Most newborns exposed to GBS will not become ill, but for those who do the results may be devastating. Two thousand newborns and infants die each year from complications of GBS infection. Annually, GBS causes infections in 12,000 newborns and infants and 48,000 infections in the mothers. Up to 50% of infants who have meningitis from GBS infection will have permanent neurologic damage. (9) GBS is the number one cause of life-threatening infections in newborns.

The treatment for GBS infection is typically dosages of antibiotics for the delivering mother and her newborn(s). Physicians would

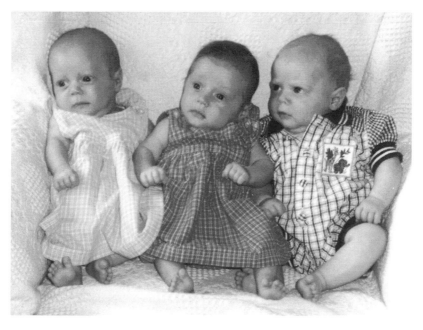

The Almonte children, South Yarmouth, Massachusetts

be reluctant to treat every woman who tests positive because they have found that usually the presence of GBS only causes problems in those pregnancies that fit a criteria for high-risk GBS infection. This high-risk criteria is as follows:

- Multiple birth
- Preterm delivery (before 37 weeks)
- Rupture of membranes for 8 or more hours prior to delivery of the baby(ies)
- High amounts of GBS **at the time of delivery** (it's difficult to know the amount of GBS at the time of delivery; the test takes too long to receive results)
- Fever in the mother during pregnancy, labor, or within 48 hours after delivery
- Prior baby with GBS
- Mother with a history of GBS in previous births
- Urinary tract infection with GBS

As you can see, multiple birth mothers typically fall into several of the high-risk criteria categories. If your physician determines that you are at risk you may be given intravenous antibiotic treatments during labor. Your babies would also receive antibiotic treatments after they're born (in some cases your babies may not need antibiotic treatment after birth).

One note for mothers of multiples. If one of your babies develops GBS infection, the other babies should be evaluated and observed. Multiples with one infected baby with GBS have a 25-fold increased risk of developing GBS infection. Be sure to discuss GBS screening with your physician. For more information on GBS, contact The Group B Strep Association (address in the Appendix).

Bacterial Vaginosis

A very common infection which often goes undiagnosed, bacterial vaginosis is known to significantly increase the risks of premature rupture of membranes and/or preterm labor and delivery. This infection happens when the bacteria normally present in the vagina multiply to an unhealthy level. An unusual odor or just excessive moisture and/or irritation may be the only symptoms, but the consequences can be significant. Be sure to report symptoms of bacterial vaginosis to your physician, and insist on being tested for the condition if you have symptoms. The test is simple and inexpensive, and the treatment is either oral antibiotics or an antibiotic cream.

Twin-Twin Transfusion Syndrome (TTTS)

TTTS is a serious complication of identical twin, triplet or higher-order multiple pregnancies in which there is one placenta for two or more babies (monochorionic placenta), and each baby is in its own sac. If there are separate placentas (dichorionic placentas) you are not at risk for this complication, even if your babies are identical. It is very important that your doctor determine if you have monochorionic or dichorionic placentas because you will need more frequent ultrasound exams to detect TTTS early in the monochorionic twins.

The twins share their blood volume in TTTS, and like later in life, twins sometimes do not share equally. One baby may get "too much" blood, and the other "too little." Mild TTTS may only cause discordant fetal weights (one baby small, the other baby normal to large) and hemoglobin concentration. In mild cases the babies usually do well. On the other hand, severe acute TTTS is a very serious complication that may result in the death of one, two, or even all babies.

Acute TTTS usually appears at 16-26 weeks gestation. The arterial circulation of one twin (donor) is connected to the venous circulation of the other twin (recipient). The donor twin transfuses the recipient twin. This abnormal circulation causes growth restriction in the donor while the recipient continues to grow normally. As acute TTTS continues, the donor will not produce enough amniotic fluid in its sac while the recipient will have too much. In some cases, the donor's amniotic volume will drop so low that the fetus becomes "stuck" against the uterine wall. This is known as the "stuck twin" phenomenon.

Left untreated, severe TTTS progresses with the mother complaining of pain from a rapidly enlarging uterus, preterm rupture of membranes, or preterm labor with the babies' delivery, usually before 26 weeks. In some cases, the one twin dies in utero (before 26 weeks), which can either cause the death of the other twin or possibly it will survive and the pregnancy can continue.

Different treatments have been tried to alleviate the problems associated with TTTS. None are completely successful. Selective fe-

4

ticide has been tried. One fetus is terminated, and the transfusing of blood from one twin to the other is stopped. There are complications associated with this because the dead fetus remains in utero while the remaining fetus is alive and growing. Another treatment tried was the surgical removal (and death) of the donor twin. This avoided the complications associated with fetal retention after a selective feticide, but surgical removal of one twin also posed many serious complications (i.e. preterm labor, preterm rupture of the membranes, infections, etc). (10)

A treatment option for TTTS that is meeting with success is a procedure called reduction amniocentesis. Reduction amniocentesis to treat severe TTTS involves removing amniotic fluid from the recipient twin's sac. Excess amniotic fluid is removed from the sac until there is a normal (or a little less than normal) amount of amniotic fluid remaining. This is done using ultrasound so that the physician may insert a needle (connected to a collecting tube) into the fetal sac to withdraw amniotic fluid. The procedure is repeated as often as necessary to maintain a normal amount of amniotic fluid in both fetal sacs (the removal of excess fluid in the recipient's sac also allows fluid to accumulate in the donor sac). This procedure allows the pregnancy to continue longer and increases the chance of the babies' survival. (11) Serial amniocentesis to treat TTTS is a promising treatment option.

Another treatment option that is showing promise is laser obliteration of the communicating blood vessels shared between the twins. This surgical procedure has met with some success in twin pregnancies and is beginning to be used in triplet pregnancies. In 1992 the procedure was successfully performed in a triplet pregnancy. The 17 minute laser surgery was performed at 18 weeks gestation. The pregnancy continued to 32 weeks gestation and all babies survived and did well. (12) Though the procedure is still considered "experimental," it is being performed successfully by some specialty centers.

When TTTS is occurring with two of the fetuses in a triplet pregnancy, the third fetus (who does not share circulation with the other two) is also at risk. Some complications of TTTS such as preterm rupture of the membranes and preterm labor would affect the entire pregnancy, not just the "twins" involved with TTTS. Death of one or more of the fetuses could also cause complications that could affect the health of the remaining living fetuses as well as the health of the mother.

If you are diagnosed with TTTS there is hope. The best resource to contact if you have been diagnosed with TTTS is the Twin To Twin

Transfusion Syndrome Foundation, Inc. This foundation provides educational, emotional, and financial support to families facing TTTS. (See Appendix for more information.)

Fetal Demise and Stillbirths in Multiple Pregnancy

Fetal demise may occur at any time during a multiple pregnancy, from the first few weeks until literally hours before delivery. With the advent of sonograms and other tools to help parents "view" their babies almost from the point of conception, there is often an extraordinary bonding that occurs very early between parents and babies. This makes such a death especially painful, whenever it occurs.

When a demise occurs in the very early weeks of pregnancy, it is often referred to as "vanishing twin syndrome." There is usually no known reason for such a death, although at times a fetus has been closely monitored for growth and development because it has been known to have had a weaker start in early gestation. In such cases, the vanishing twin is usually reabsorbed or spontaneously aborted without causing problems for the remaining babies. In a literature review, 21.2% of the twin pregnancies studied had a vanishing twin. (13)

Later in pregnancy, loss can occur for a number of reasons including twin to twin transfusion (TTTS), intra-uterine growth restriction (IUGR), cord entanglement, fetal anomalies, placental insufficiency, or other unknown complications. When a fetal demise occurs in mid or late pregnancy, the pregnancy is usually managed without interruption unless or until the physician feels the remaining babies are sufficiently mature to deliver. The pregnancy usually continues without problems for the remaining fetuses until time of delivery. However, the remaining fetuses are typically closely monitored for any signs of distress so that they can be delivered at any hint of problems.

At times, a baby dies very late in pregnancy, sometimes even hours before a planned delivery. Such a demise is usually attributed to a placental breakdown that deprives the baby of needed oxygen and/or nutrition. Such loss can usually be avoided by physicians performing regular (usually twice weekly) biophysical profiles late in pregnancy to ascertain the general overall well being of each infant. For this reason, many physicians plan to deliver multiple infants before such an occurrence would be likely to happen.

4

Multiple Loss, Multiple Grief

When one infant in a multiple pregnancy dies either prior to birth or afterwards, the natural grieving process for parents may be very difficult. While the parents may be anticipating or celebrating the health of their remaining baby or babies, *they have lost a baby.* Family and friends may not understand their grief because of the remaining healthy baby(s). Regardless of the fact that there are multiple babies in the pregnancy, each baby is as precious as the other(s) to the parents involved, and each must be grieved for regardless of the health of the other(s). Watching the remaining children grow is an everyday reminder of the missing baby, and often intensifies and prolongs the grieving process.

For families who have lost one or more of their multiple birth infants, there is networking and sympathy available through The Triplet Connection. We have many families who, having suffered a loss, have asked to be resources to others who have also experienced such a loss. No one can understand this experience like someone who has endured it. There are also national self-help organizations for families who have suffered an infant loss (see Appendix).

Conclusion

The complications we have discussed may seem overwhelming. It is important to realize that many women have multiple pregnancies that are closely monitored and have few, if any complications; however, it is equally important to be aware of all complications that *may* occur. Knowing about potential complications can often help you avoid problems. By being aware of warning signs and reporting them early, patients can often avoid serious crises situations.

Each year physicians are learning more and more about the management of multiple pregnancies. Working closely with your physician will give you the best possible care and will help you deliver healthy babies. Taking the time to learn about your pregnancy and taking the best possible care of yourself is your biggest contribution to a healthy pregnancy and a good outcome.

Endnotes

(1) Arias F, MD, PhD, Delayed delivery of multifetal pregnancies with preterm rupture of membranes in the second trimester. Am J Obstet Gynecol 1994;170(5):1233-1237.

(2) The Triplet Connection Newsletter, 1993:Vol 10, No. 3, p. 13.

(3) The Triplet Connection Newsletter, 1993:Vol 10, No. 4, p. 1, 33.

(4) Dyson DC et al. Prevention of preterm birth in high-risk patients: The role of education and provider contact versus home uterine monitoring. Am J Obstet Gynecol 1991;164(3):756-762.

(5) The Triplet Connection Newsletter, 1992:Vol 10, No. 3, p. 13.

(6) The Triplet Connection Newsletter, 1992:Vol. 9, No. 2, p. 16.

(7) Gunderson E.P. Gestational Diabetes: Diabetes that Develops During Pregnancy. California Diabetes and Pregnancy Program. Children's Hospital, San Francisco.

(8) Ibid.

(9) Noya FJD, Baker CJ. Prevention of Group B Streptococcal Infection. Pediatric Infections. 1992;6;1:41-55.

(10) Urig AM, Simpson GF, Elliott JP, Clewell WH. Twin-Twin Transfusion Syndrome. The Surgical Removal of One Twin as a Treatment Option. Fetal Ther 1988;3:185-188.

(11) Elliott J, Urig MA, Clewell WH. Aggressive Therapeutic Amniocentesis for Treatment of Twin-Twin Transfusion Syndrome. Obstet & Gyn 1991;7;4:537-540.

(12) Milwaulkee Sentinel. Times 3: Unique laser surgery triples mother's joy. November 10, 1992. and Contact! Employee Communication for Milwaukee Medical Complex. November 19, 1992, Vol 3, No. 24.

(13) Sabbagha RE. Pregnancy dating and evaluation by ultrasonography. In Multiple Pregnancy. Epidemiology, Gestation & Perinatal Outcome. Keith LG, Papiernik E, Keith DM, Luke B. Parthenon Publishing Group. New York, London. 1995.

The Atkinson family, Pageland, South Carolina

After the Birth

Breastfeeding

Breastfeeding three or more is not like breastfeeding two or less. An acquaintance kindly pointed this out to me. "You're not planning to nurse them, are you?" When I answered that I did indeed intend to do just that, his reply was, "Well, how are you going to do that? You only have two of those," as he gestured towards my breasts.

—CG in Colorado (1)

Many women, after learning they're expecting higher-order multiples, completely give up on the idea of possibly breastfeeding their infants. It often seems like an overwhelming possibility; after all, we have only two breasts! What do you do with the third (or fourth, etc.) baby? How can a mother possibly have adequate milk supply to care for the needs of triplets or more? How can she possibly have the time or energy to do anything else if she spends all her time breastfeeding three or more babies? Such questions sometimes plague expectant mothers, and they often feel there is no way possible that they can breastfeed whether or not they may have previously wanted to try.

Breastmilk always has and always will be the most perfect milk available for babies. Specially formulated by a mother's body for her infants, there's no better way to give your babies a more healthy start in life. In providing breastmilk for babies, a mother is gifting her babies with her antibodies, helping protect them from allergies, decreasing their chances of developing ear infections and other childhood diseases, as well as feeding them the most healthy and nourishing "formula" known to man.

But, you may ask, is it really feasible to do? Am I a failure or am I letting my babies down if I decide *not* to try to breastfeed? What if I try, only to fail? What if I try and decide this is not for me? Is there any way for me to grow one or more breasts between now and when my babies are born?

Well, there's no way for you to grow another breast, and you are *not* a worse mother if you do not breastfeed your babies. There *are* options for breastfeeding, though, whether you're a mother of triplets, quadruplets, or even more. Many of our mothers of higher-order multiples have exclusively breastfed their infants for months to years. Many have *partially* breastfed for months to years. Many have provided their breast milk for the first few weeks only – just long enough to give their babies a good start. Some have provided their milk just while babies were in the hospital, or just while they were having problems due to prematurity, etc.

Babies who are born prematurely can often benefit greatly from being given their mother's breast milk. Often, if they are struggling with problems due to prematurity, the neonatologists and nurses will literally beg a mother to provide her milk, even if only for a short time. Breast milk can sometimes help prematurely-born babies avoid many potential digestion-related problems. Dr. Boyd Goetzman, director of Neonatology at UC Davis Medical Center in Sacramento, CA, and a member of The Triplet Connection Scientific Advisory Board, reminds all mothers of preemies that the best way to help prevent NEC (Necrotizing Enterocolitis), a potentially fatal intestinal disease, is to provide breast milk for premature infants.

Premature infants given small amounts of breast milk shortly after birth can tolerate regular feedings more quickly. A study of 70 premature infants weighing less than 2.5 pounds found that breast milk stimulated the production of lactase, an enzyme that digests lactose, the sugar in milk. (2) The study states that infants fed only intravenously, the common practice, took longer to produce lactase. Lactase production is an early sign that the gastrointestinal system is maturing.

If you have a desire to breastfeed your infants, do not be discouraged by those who will try to convince you that it is impossible. We have literally thousands of mothers of triplets or more who have been extremely successful with breastfeeding their infants. Contact The Triplet Connection for resource people if and when you feel you need encouragement or tips. Contact the LeLeche League International for a copy of their excellent book, *The Womanly Art of Breastfeeding*, as well as their resources for breastfeeding multiple infants. Such books are most helpful, particularly if read while you are still pregnant.

If you are undecided about breastfeeding, there is something you can do. Use a breastpump every day from as soon after the babies are born as possible – at least two or more times each day – until you are firmly decided. That way, your milk will still be established if and when you wish to try breastfeeding. Some women have kept the window of opportunity open in this way until their lives were somewhat settled, and then decided (sometimes weeks after giving birth) to begin breastfeeding – and they've been successful. It is relatively easy to stop milk production by using the pump less each day until you are no longer producing milk.

Until your babies are well and strong, it is often very difficult to directly breastfeed. If you can persevere through the weeks or months until they are strong enough to effectively nurse, the rewards are great. When they are able to "latch" on well and you're feeling comfortable and confident, it's time to begin nursing two babies simultaneously.

The best way to accomplish dual breastfeeding is to sit on a couch or bed, where you have plenty of room on both sides of you for your babies to lie facing away from one another. Prop your feet so that you knees are up in a bend (a coffee table works well, or a recliner is great), your legs providing support for your babies. Position a pillow beneath each baby, so that you do not have to hold the weight of your babies as you nurse and your hands are free to rearrange them. Another effective position that works well is to hold the first baby in the conventional manner, with head at your elbow and body facing across your body. The head of the next baby lies on the tummy of the first, both bodies facing the same direction.

If you've never breastfed a baby before, you may not be aware that the first weeks of breastfeeding are usually not very rewarding. Babies are needing to learn to nurse well, you're leaking milk, you may be engorged and uncomfortable, and there is some general frustration in the whole process. Also, while you're needing to utilize the electric pump (if you need to), the experience is anything but joyous! Have patience (and faith in yourself and in nature). If you can see things through the first sometimes miserable weeks, you will suddenly find yourself truly enjoying the experience. You'll stop leaking, the babies will become expert nursers, you'll simultaneously nurse two at a time, and you'll do it in not much more time than it would take to prepare bottles (and at tremendous cost savings).

In time, your babies will "explore" one another as they nurse, and more often than not they'll find one another's hands and hold hands as you nurse them (now, if that doesn't melt your heart, I don't know what will!). Many mothers nursed their third (or third and fourth) infant(s) after finishing with the first two, or they had pumped milk ready for someone else to feed as they nursed, or they simply fed the last baby formula. Remember you can always just nurse one of your infants each feeding time, providing mom's milk just every third feeding if nursing all three or four does not work for you.

If you choose not to breastfeed, please do not feel guilty or inadequate. Breastfeeding is definitely not for everyone, and you must do what is best for your particular situation. Most babies seem to thrive on formula, but no babies thrive without love. The most important "nutrient" your babies can receive is constant love from you!

5

Endnotes

(1) *The Triplet Connection Newsletter*, 1996:Vol. 13, No. 1, p. 25.

(2) *Shulman, RJ, Schanler, RJ, Lau, C, Heitkemper, M, Ou, C-N, Smith, EO. Early feeding, feeding tolerance, and lactase activity in preterm infants. J Pediatr 1998, 645-649.*

Bringing Babies Home

Afer two months, all of our babies finally came home to us . . . Our lives turned upside down several times during that first year . . .

—ES in Tennessee (1)

It seems like only yesterday that I was giving birth to my oldest, middle and youngest child all within three minutes. Now, they are beginning the journey to independence. I wouldn't want to change a minute of the last few years, except maybe to hold onto their childhood just a little longer.

—SC in Montana (2)

Congratulations! You're bringing your babies home! For many parents, especially those who have had infants spend significant time in the hospital after their birth, bringing babies home is a much-anticipated time. Now is the time to settle in with your children.

Because most multiple pregnancies resulted in a c-section delivery and preterm babies, there are some issues to be faced by new parents of triplets or more.

Most parents feel totally unprepared when their babies come home. Three tiny babies and all their supplies can initially be an overwhelming sight! Do try to have help available. Make a schedule, and let friends and relatives who express a desire to help out fill themselves in on your schedule. This one word of advice: scheduling help has provided the kind of steady, dependable assistance that is still around many months after multiples are born. Demanding and exciting though it is to have your babies at home, it is good to be prepared for their arrival with all the necessary help and paraphernalia required to care for their needs.

Depression

Having just been through an emotional, uncomfortable, apprehension-filled pregnancy followed by major surgery, and then often faced with preterm infants, mothers (and even fathers) sometimes find themselves in a state of depression following the birth of the babies. Fortunately, this does not happen to many, but when it does it is often a shock and a great disappointment to realize that at a time when they should be feeling the most exquisite joy, they are instead feeling the greatest sense of uncertainty and depression. If you find yourself in this situation, take heart; it is probably very temporary, and is normal. It may not be depression at all, but simply sleep deprivation and exhaustion. If you feel you are *unduly* depressed or unable to cope with your feelings, be sure to let your doctor know. Talk with others who might reassure you. Seek professional help, if necessary. Do not feel ashamed or feel you are "unworthy" of professional help. There is a national post-partum support group offering resources and referrals for those who find themselves in need of help (see Appendix).

Getting Organized

Most families report that organization is the key to their survival during the first few months of their multiples' infancy. Organization saves time (looking for pacifiers, bottles, blankets, etc) and is a life saver for many families. The first task after (or shortly be-

5

fore) bringing babies home is to begin acquiring all the supplies you'll need. Many parents are reluctant to do this well in advance because of the uncertainty of the outcome of their pregnancies. A note of encouragement when acquiring baby equipment and supplies: the birth of triplets or more is an exciting time! That excitement catches on! You may be surprised at the generosity of people. Many couples report that family and friends were coming out of the woodwork with offers to help with babies, donate cribs, high-chairs, car seats, clothing, etc. This is the time to gratefully *accept* these offers. Also, consignment shops and used children's clothing shops are a godsend for parents of multiples.

Infant Car Seats

You must bring your babies home from the hospital in infant car seats, so plan ahead and have the correct number on hand. Many hospitals or local social service agencies will loan or rent car seats for you to use. You will eventually want your own infant car seats, but remember that your babies will probably be very small when you bring them home. It may be more economical for you to borrow or rent the initial car seats and purchase seats for larger babies that will last longer for you. Before you purchase a car seat, be sure to try buckling and unbuckling it—a seat with a handier buckle may cost a little more, but may be worth the extra money for the convenience it will bring. Also, padded inserts made for car seats will help tiny babies be more comfortable, and will prop their necks and heads (an important safety feature). Be very sure that the model of carseats you use, whether new or used, meets current safety standards.

Cribs

You may not need three cribs initially. Newborn triplets often sleep better together in one crib. As they grow, they'll graduate into their own cribs. Many parents find that having a crib in one room and a porta-crib or bassinet in another room for a fussy baby is a must. One note: if you're contemplating using second-hand cribs, make sure that they are safe – corner posts of the cribs should be flush with the rest of the crib so that toddlers can't catch their clothing on the posts and strangle themselves. Check all screws in new and used cribs; loose screws are a potential choking hazard. Don't use the cribs if the bars are widely spaced (infants can get caught between the bars and strangle). Check the fit of the mattress in the crib. Loose-fitting mattresses pose a danger, as an infant can become wedged between the mattress and the crib. Also be aware that bumper pads must fit properly. Loose, sagging bumper pads can be a suffocation hazard if an infant (especially a tiny infant) becomes pushed up against loose bumper pads.

Bookshelves, Dressers, Etc.

As your multiples grow, free-standing dressers and other heavy furniture can become hazardous to your children. One toddler may not be able to cause a dresser or bookshelf to tip over, but multiple toddlers climbing on shelves or in drawers may cause the furniture to tip onto the children. Serious injuries and even death have resulted from furniture falling onto multiple birth children. Bolt bookshelves, dressers, etc., to the wall to prevent such disastrous accidents from happening.

Baby Bottles

Be sure to ask the nurses in the hospital to save all the bottles and nipples used for your babies while in the hospital. Take them home, wash them, and store them in plastic zip-lock bags to be used when you need them. In a few days time, you can have as many bottles as you will need to last until your babies are ready for larger ones.

Charting

Many parents chart essential daily information about each baby. A clipboard with a chart on it is quick and easy to find. Make a chart for each child, put his/her name on the top and then have a list of essential information: last feeding, amount the baby ate, last diaper change, last bowel movement, last nap, any concerns you have about the child, etc. After taking care of three or more babies all day and night, it may surprising how you can lose track of who's eaten when, etc. A chart will help you keep track of that information so that you will notice if one child is constipated, not eating very much, or not sleeping much, etc. This information will help you to keep your children healthy. (See Appendix Articles and Charts.)

Organized Feeding

If you're bottle-feeding, devise a method of making up bottles. If you are breast feeding, you will want to organize yourself with pumping and storing milk. Either way, it's very frustrating to be trying to get three hungry babies fed when you're not organized. Some parents make up a day's worth of bottles all at once; others measure out formula and add the water when it's feeding time (then you can just add room temperature water and the bottle is ready). Remember, heating bottles in a microwave can be unsafe since the formula may heat unevenly and burn your baby's mouth. Always check the temperature of the formula before feeding babies.

Getting Help

You may want to consider bringing in outside help during certain hours of the day or night. If money is an issue, ask family members, friends or people from your community or local church to help you out for those first weeks. Sometimes family members who would

The Grimm children, Manhasset, New York

love to be of help but are unable to do so will be happy, if asked, to contribute financially toward paid help. This gives them an opportunity to help ensure the assistance they would be giving if they were able to do so themselves.

Caring for three or more babies, especially preterm babies, can be demanding. Think about having extra help during critical times such as during bath time, visits to your pediatrician, etc. An extra set of hands during these times can be a godsend! If you have other children you may want to schedule extra help while your other children will be around. This will leave some "Mom" or "Dad" time for them while helpers are taking care of the babies.

If you find it extremely difficult to ask for needed help, try to keep this in mind: you are not asking for help for your own convenience or luxury, but for the quality of life of your babies. If it is too difficult for you to do the asking, try to involve a close friend. Let her be the one to keep a "schedule" of helpers. Then, when people ask to help, let them know that your friend is keeping a schedule of help. Let them call your friend (or have your friend call them) to schedule the help they would like to contribute. It is surprising how often people truly do want to help if they just know how they can be of service. This also gives them the opportunity to volunteer for the days or hours which they can fit into their schedules.

5

Locating Needed Items for Babies

Take some time to go to a bookstore or search the Internet for information on the latest baby products. Some will become invaluable to you. If you want to purchase a twin, triplet or quadruplet stroller, information is available through the Triplet Connection to purchase one at a discount.

Baby Supplies

Your life will be much easier if you have enough of everything such as diapers (cloth or disposable), bottles (if you choose to bottle feed), receiving blankets, sleepers, bibs, etc. If you're wondering just what you'll need to "outfit" your babies, here are some suggestions:

- **Three or more cribs or porta-cribs.** One is often used in the beginning, but you'll eventually need one for each child.
- **At least three changes of sheets per crib.** Mattress pads may be used, but receiving blankets work very well, too.
- **At least five receiving blankets per baby.** You can also use additional receiving blankets if you plan to use them for mattress pads.
- **At least two lightweight and one heavier blanket per baby.**
- **Pacifiers.** Most parents have found that very tiny babies won't take a pacifier. Often this is because the nipple is too large and/or hard. Look for pacifiers for preterm babies. They're smaller than usual and softer. Buy about 12, if you can find them!
- **Bottles.** The number you will need depends upon how often your babies are needing to be fed and whether or not you are breast feeding. If you can have a full days' supply of bottles and nipples (with three to six to spare), it is sure a help. Because some babies may be on a two-hour feeding schedule in the beginning (if they're small babies), you may require 36 bottles and nipples a day for triplets. Remember to get them from the hospital while your babies are hospitalized!
- **Cloth Diapers.** Whether you decide to use your own cloth diapers, a diaper service, or disposable diapers, you will definitely need some cloth diapers of your own. Cloth diapers are handy for use as burp pads, etc. For those who diaper their babies with cloth diapers, you will need about five dozen diapers in the beginning.
- **Disposable diapers.** If you're planning on using disposable diapers, check out different brands to find the features that you like best. Local stores may be willing to donate or give you a discount on disposable diapers. Also, some diaper companies will give coupons for the purchase of their diapers (check the New Mom's Baby Products & Gifts List, available from The Triplet Connection).
- **Clothing.** Many parents have found that the easiest, most comfortable item for new babies was the terry snap-up sleeper. At least four sleepers per baby would be wonderful. The advantage of these sleepers is that they are perfectly acceptable for day or night. Depending on the weather, a coat or sweater apiece will be needed.
- **Strollers.** After your babies are past the newborn stage, a stroller is a must. Perego, RunAbout and Baby Jogger strollers are avail-

able through Janet Bleyl, an independent dealer, at a reduced cost. Contact her at (209) 474-3073, P.O. Box 99414, Stockton, CA 95209 for more information.

- **Playpens.** Playpens simply do not work for triplets or more, because the area provided is too small. Expandable "corrals" are more practical. These "corrals" can be used to safely enclose a play area that is big enough for all your babies.

- **Swings.** Battery-operated or wind-up swings may be invaluable. Many parents prefer battery-operated swings as they are quieter and there is no need for winding. Because they're used for a relatively short time, it may be more economical to borrow one or two of them.

- **High Chairs.** You'll need one high chair per baby. Be sure to get high chairs with safety straps and bars between the legs to hold babies securely in place. If you're purchasing high chairs, check out how they latch, adjust, etc. Cumbersome buckles and adjustments will become frustrating when you multiply the hassle times three or more. Some mothers have preferred the attachable chairs that are secured to the table – they take up less room.

> **There is rarely a dull moment when you're living with three babies, but we wouldn't trade a minute of this chaos.**
>
> **—KC in Georgia (3)**

Here are a few tips that will make your life easier when you're home with your multiples:

- Setting up a full-sized crib in the main living portion of your house, as well as in your bedroom saves steps and adds extra convenience when taking care of your babies. Parents report that they liked the convenience of a crib nearby, and their babies were happy together in the crib. The babies quickly adjusted to the noise of the household and slept peacefully during the day in the main area of the house. At night, they slept in one crib in the bedroom area. By the time they were ready to be separated into individual cribs (usually when they begin rolling over and moving around more), they were ready to be moved into their own room. Many babies seem to love to be together, sharing body warmth and comfort. Amazingly, their cries do not seem to awaken one another, and it becomes good conditioning for later – their cries still won't bother one another.

- Diaper rash is often quickly cleared up by drying baby's bottoms with a hair blow dryer, turned on low. Keep one at the changing area, but out of reach of babies and small children.

- Some parents find that setting up "diapering stations" in different rooms in their house is a help. Time can be saved when you don't have to go up or down stairs and from one end of the house to the other to change a diaper.

- Until you move the crib from the main living area of your house, use it as a changing table. Just set the mattress high enough for your comfort. Later, it's great to have a changing area where your babies will play.

- As for new baby care, we've all developed methods of operation, but one lesson was quickly learned by all. When working with triplets or more, a schedule is not an option but a necessity! You might be able to leave one or two babies asleep for long enough to feed the first two, but the object of your schedule must be to get them sleeping together in order to provide yourself with some time when you are not "in demand." In other words, it is not necessary to have a *time* schedule to awaken your babies, etc., but if one awakens to be fed, it's best to awaken the others soon afterwards. Spend special time with babies individually by keeping one up for a little longer, or awakening one a little sooner, but do try to get your babies' sleeping schedule coordinated.

- Don't worry about a daily bath. A sponge bath every other day will do nicely, and their skin won't be as dry.

- Make priorities for every day, remembering that in the beginning your first priority will be your babies. Some days in the beginning will be a bit overwhelming – which is an understatement! Keep in mind that this, too, will pass! Every week and month will get to be a little easier. The first six months are definitely the hardest, and month by month, things get progressively easier to handle.

- Allow time for yourself. Try to get out with your spouse at least once a week. Have a friend – or two babysitters – watch the babies for long enough to let you get away for a change of pace.

- If you find your babies are coming home with monitors, network with other families who have done the same.

- Take one day at a time – sometimes one hour at a time. You are in a *temporary* situation.

- Check with neighbors or friends who have junior high or high school age children. You may be able to hire someone at that age for a reasonable rate. Children that age may not be responsible enough to be left alone with your babies, but they can be a "mother's helper" while you're there. They can also help with household chores, laundry, etc.

- A cordless phone has been incredibly convenient for households with multiples.

- Baby intercoms are also very helpful. Make sure you follow the manufacturer's directions for use. Placing baby monitors in the crib may cause a fire hazard.

5

Endnotes

(1) The Triplet Connection Newsletter, 1995:Vol. 13, No. 3, p.28.

(2) The Triplet Connection Newsletter, 1995:Vol. 13, No. 1, p.9.

(3) The Triplet Connection Newsletter, 1996:Vol. 13, No. 3, p.29.

For Safety's Sake

Health and safety considerations for any infant or toddler can be a challenge. Multiples present some unique challenges that many parents are unaware of. Three infants or toddlers can work together and get themselves into all kinds of situations. Many of these situations are humorous and will become family stories. However, some situations are deadly, with tragic results. Some families have experienced serious injury or death of one or more of their multiples through situations that would often have been safe with only one child, but which are unsafe with three (or more). These tragedies make us realize that there are unique safety considerations for families with multiples. There are also some health concerns that parents of infants, especially preterm infants, should be aware of.

The following list represents a wide variety of health and safety issues that you will want to consider. Please read each topic carefully, and don't delay taking actions to make your home as safe as possible for your multiples:

Respiratory Syncytial Virus (RSV)

RSV is a respiratory infection that usually begins with a "cold." Multiples with immature lungs and respiratory systems are especially at risk for complications of RSV. This virus can progress to pneumonia and to the point where the infant/toddler cannot breath. Apnea (failure to breathe) and Sudden Infant Death Syndrome (SIDS) is also associated with RSV. The infection can be deadly, quickly progressing to the point where infants must be placed on respirators to keep them alive. RSV can progress so quickly that an infant or toddler can die before reaching the doctor or hospital. RSV occurs in epidemics, rarely in infants younger than six weeks old, and is extremely contagious.

What do you need to watch for? "Fever in any child less than ten to twelve weeks old requires medical evaluation as soon as possible. Poor feeding, listlessness, or extreme irritability are also worrisome. In addition, here are three keys of respiratory difficulty that you can recognize at home:

1. **Rapid Breathing** – The normal infant (less than three months of age) breathes 24-36 times a minute. In the case of pneumonia, this may rise to 40-60 times a minute.

2. **Nasal Flaring** – Many sick infants will flare (or expand) both nostrils with every breath. Healthy infants will not.

3. **Retractions** – In an effort to provide as much air as possible for oxygen-starved lungs, a child with respiratory distress will suck in the soft-tissue between and below the ribs with each breath. This is apparent if you stare at their chest, and should not occur in a healthy infant."(1)

If your multiples or other children are suffering from a cold, keep a close watch on their health. If your infant exhibits any of the above signs or their cold worsens, seek medical help immediately. If you feel your baby is in significant distress, seek emergency services rather than driving to the hospital.

Overheating Babies

Many parents worry that their babies will not be warm enough. One problem with preterm babies is that they cannot maintain their body temperature – in short, they're cold. This may lead parents to overdress their infants. Often parents don't realize that *overheating* their babies is a concern. Dressing babies too warmly has been associated with sudden infant death syndrome. Suffocation is also a threat due to the layers of clothing that the infant may become entangled in. Many physicians recommend dressing your infants as warmly (or coolly) as you are dressed. With preterm infants it is imperative that you ask your neonatologist about how to dress them. Get his/her recommendations so that your babies will not only be comfortable, but safe too.

Immunizations

Life is hectic with multiples, especially during the first several months. Don't let a busy schedule keep you from making (and keeping) appointments to have your infants immunized. Their lives may depend on this! Be aware that the usual immunization schedule may be adjusted if your infants are low birthweight. For example, your pediatrician may wait until your infants are at a certain weight, rather than a certain age, to begin immunizing them. Your doctor will be able to let you know what the immunization schedule will be for your children. One other hint: have only the baby that is receiving the immunization in the room at the time it's done. Mayhem may break loose with the waiting babies when they witness the distressed cries of their sibling who has just received a shot!

Lead Ingestion

Older homes may have paint and pipes that contain lead. Make sure your children are not eating any chipped paint. More importantly, if you live in an older home, do not mix baby formula or cook using *hot tap* water. The hot water running through the pipes of your home can be contaminated with lead. Chronic lead ingestion by children can cause mental retardation.

Water Temperature

Parents of small children may want to turn the water temperature down on their water heaters. Water heater temperatures can be set high enough to scald a child. Check with your physician or hospital for water heater temperature recommendations in homes with small children.

Electrical Outlets

Safety covers for electrical outlets make sense for homes with small children. However, some of the safety covers are small and easily removed. Check to make sure that the covers fit tightly. Better yet, look for safety covers that screw onto a specially-designed switch plate and are large enough so that they can't be choked on.

Home Safety

Homes with multiples require extra childproofing. Dressers and bookshelves should be bolted to walls. One toddler climbing on a dresser or bookshelf may not pose a safety risk, but three or more toddlers climbing do. The Triplet Connection has received tragic news of multiples who have died by suffocation when toddlers have tipped a dresser or bookshelf onto themselves. This situation can be especially dangerous in the children's bedroom where a tipping dresser or bookshelf can push a child facedown onto a mattress, suffocating the child(ren). It is especially important to make the bedrooms safe because toddlers often play there without close supervision. Some parents have had to bolt toddler beds onto a board or to the floor so that their multiples can't pick up one end of a bed and tip the bed and mattress onto themselves. Padding sharp corners of tables, etc., is also recommended. It will save a lot of bumps and bruises, but will also help prevent falls that cause lacerations requiring sutures. Additionally, watch for any items which may be tipped over by children or may be hazardous outdoors, in the garage – literally anywhere the children will be.

5

Strangulation Dangers

Parents should check throughout their home for *anything* that could pose a strangling risk to their multiples. Belts hanging in closets, window blind cords, looped telephone cords, decorative ribbons, *anything* with a loop can potentially strangle a child.

Choking Hazards

Again, parents should check their homes for anything small that is within the reach of infants and toddlers. This may be quite a challenge if there are older siblings in the family who have toys and small parts to toys that a younger sibling could choke on. As mentioned previously, electrical safety covers can be a choking hazard if the infant or child can remove the cover. Latex balloons can break and children can choke on them. Loose screws in cribs or other furniture can be picked up by a child and choked on. Uncooked macaroni, often used for toddlers to string (like beads), has also caused choking death. Beads, coins, small toys, the list is endless – all are choking hazards. It may seem like an impossible task to keep these things out of an infant or child's reach, but not doing so can be deadly.

Glass Windows

Some parents of multiples have replaced toddler bedroom windows with safety glass. Again, one toddler is more likely to be safe in a bedroom, but three or more toddlers can help one another climb and subsequently be pushed through a window. Other parents have chosen to cover windows, glass in bookshelves, etc., to prevent their young children from harming one another or themselves.

Car Seats

Surveys have shown that many infant/children's car seats are not properly installed. Common errors are things such as not using a locking clip on certain retractable seatbelts, not having the seat in the proper position (facing forward or back), etc. Improperly installed car seats are a safety hazard. Take the time to read the directions and install them properly! But most importantly, *use* car seats for your infants and children! Countless deaths each year are directly attributable to lack of car seat use.

Room Barriers

"Corrals" and other room barriers can be extremely helpful to parents of multiples. Both can help set apart a portion of a room (or whole room) that you're sure is safe for your children. One warning about older gates and corrals: the gates that expand forming a diamond pattern can be dangerous for small infants and children (the child's head can get caught in the "diamonds"). Another thing to keep in mind with gates in doorways is to watch that the children can't climb, even partially, over the gate. If the gate is at the top of a set of stairs, the child can take a dangerous fall. Sometimes specially-installed, removable barriers may be necessary to insure the safety of your multiples. They're worth the added expense and peace of mind.

Infant CPR

Most hospitals and/or your local American Red Cross offer infant CPR courses. Taking an infant CPR course is a good idea for anyone, but is especially recommended for parents of preterm babies.

Shaken Baby Syndrome

Never shake or hit a baby. Brief shaking can cause permanent brain damage or death. Every parent feels she/he is losing control at times of great stress and frustration caused by lack of sleep or crying infants or children, etc. If you ever feel you are losing control, take your baby/babies to a safe place (crib, playpen, etc.). Leave the room and close the door. Walk outside if necessary. Stay away for the few minutes it will take you to calm down and regain control. Rough play, such as tossing a baby into the air, can also cause permanent damage.

Potential Child Abuse

If you ever feel you need help to regain control, call Childhelp USA (800-4-A-CHILD). You will be helped immediately by a trained telephone counselor 24 hours a day. They will help you find a solution. This service is provided free of charge, and your call is anonymous. No one will report your call or in any way jeopardize your position as a parent. To report child abuse or to find resources for help, you can also call The National Committee to Prevent Child Abuse (800-CHILDREN). This is a place to call for information to be received later, not a 24-hour resource.

One Final Note

One day, so soon you won't believe it, your children will not need all the extra equipment and safety features that they require while they're small. They'll be out driving your car while you're peacefully watching a movie in your too-quiet house (telephone in hand, beeper in pocket, tranquilizers nearby).

The Albyn family, Littleton, Colorado

Endnotes

(1) Sainsbury S., Viral Pneumonia of Infants. The Triplet Connection Newsletter.1995:Vol.12, No. 4, p. 5.

Enjoying the Miracle

Multiple births are a joy and a miracle worth all the effort they require — from conception through adulthood! It *is* possible to have healthy, happy triplets or higher order multiples. Certainly more effort is required both on the part of the expectant parents and the managing physician, but success is most likely when motivated, informed parents-to-be combine with positive, conscientious physicians in a partnership focused on promoting the best possible outcome.

For those of us who have had the opportunity to welcome three, four or more babies simultaneously into our lives, we can testify that the experience is nothing short of a miracle! It *is* do-able and accomplishable! Truly, our beautiful children have been worth every effort. They *are* our greatest treasures!

The Cotham children, Austin, Texas

Appendix

SSI Can Help Pay for Cost of Care for Smallest Infants

Contributed by Steve Potter, Social Security
Administration Public Information Specialist

Thanks to the miracles of modern medical science, today many preterm and low birthweight infants who previously would have been unable to survive now live and thrive. But the cost of modern medical techniques and services is high and, for parents with inadequate or no health insurance, it can be both a financial and emotional strain. The Supplemental Security Income (SSI) program may provide some financial help for these low birthweight babies – a benefit of the SSI program that is not widely known.

The SSI program pays benefits to people with low income and limited assets if they are age 65 or older, blind, or have a disability. Under the program's rules, very low birthweight babies automatically meet Social Security's definition of disability until they are at least a year old.

Infants born before the 38th week of pregnancy are considered preterm, and if they weigh less than 2,500 grams (about 5-1/2 pounds), they are classified as low birthweight. Preterm infants weighing less than 1,200 grams (2 pounds, 10 ounces) at birth are considered disabled. Preterm infants weighing between 1,200 and 2,000 grams (about 4 pounds, 6 ounces) at birth may be considered disabled if they are small for their gestational age and/or have serious medical problems.

Low birthweight babies generally tend to remain in a hospital's intensive care unit for an extended period of time. *The Supplemental Security Income rules don't count the parents' income and resources in determining the child's SSI eligibility or payment amount until the month following the month the child comes home to live with his/her parents.* Many of these children remain eligible for SSI after they return home if they and their parents have limited income and resources.

In many states, a child's eligibility for SSI can automatically establish his or her eligibility for Medicaid. Medicaid and SSI coverage can improve access to other available services, such as physician visits and medical equipment that the child may need after leaving the hospital.

For more information about the SSI program and children, call Social Security's toll-free telephone number, (800) 772-1213, any business day between 7:00 am and 7:00 pm. The best times to call are early in the morning, late in the afternoon, late in the week, and toward the end of the month. Or, contact your local Social Security office. Ask for the leaflet, <u>Social Security and SSI For Children With Disabilites</u>.

Note from The Triplet Connection: Our families have found that this SSI benefit is **not** retroactive, and must, therefore, be applied for as soon as possible after the birth of the babies. You can, by telephone, file an "intent to file" as soon as the babies are born. We have been told that it is important to get the name of the person to whom you are speaking, the date, time, etc., to back up your original intent to file.

6

Fibronectin Testing in the Management of Triplets and Quadruplets

by John P. Elliott, M.D.

The most common problem causing a poor outcome in triplet/quadruplet pregnancies is preterm labor leading to preterm delivery. It is often very difficult to make the diagnosis because the symptoms you feel as a patient are non-specific (backache, pelvic pressure, increased vaginal discharge, etc.), contractions are difficult to detect, and cervical change is not uniform. Failure to make the proper diagnosis and to start aggressive treatment may lead to premature delivery. Additional tests are needed to improve the accuracy of the diagnosis. Fetal Fibronectin (fFN) is the latest test approved by the FDA to help patients and physicians to predict risk of preterm delivery.

What is fFN?

fFN is a protein that is made by the amniotic membranes and the inner layer of the uterus. It functions as a "glue" to attach the membranes to the uterus. It is found in all pregnancies and can be easily sampled from the secretions found in a woman's vagina. At about 22 weeks, the normal membranes are completely sealed and no fFN is released into the vagina until about 2 to 3 weeks prior to delivery at term (40 weeks). Detecting fFN in the vaginal secretions between 24 and 34 weeks indicates an increased chance that delivery will occur prematurely.

Studies have shown that in patients either at risk for preterm delivery (but not currently in labor) or patients in current preterm labor with the cervix dilated less than 3 cm, fFN testing can help to determine risk of delivery. In singleton pregnancies, if the fFN test is negative, the risk of delivery in the next two weeks is less than 1%. However, if the fFN test is positive, the chance of delivery in the next two weeks is 16%.

How Is the Test Done?

Your physician will do a speculum exam (like a pap smear) and use a Q-tip to obtain a sample from your vagina. The test takes between 6-36 hours to run depending on the lab. It is either positive (bad) or negative (good).

How Does the Test Help Me?

A negative test is reassuring that you will probably not deliver in the next two weeks. You must still continue bedrest and all precautions, but management might be less intense. A positive test alerts the physician to expect problems. Steroids should generally be given, bedrest enforced, tocolysis may be indicated, and hospitalization might also be appropriate. There have not been any studies to tell physicians what to do with a positive test, so that care must be individualized.

Is fFN the Same in Triplets/Quadruplets?

Our early experience in Phoenix with 13 patients (1 quint, 5 quads, 7 triplets) showed 6/13 (46%) developing a positive fFN prior to delivery. The average age of delivery for six fFN positive patients was 29.8 weeks, compared to 32.9 weeks for fFN negative patients (7). The positive fFN patients delivered 17.2 days average after a + test (singleton delivery was 25 days average after a + test). It appears that high order multiples have positive results more frequently than singleton pregnancies and the time to delivery is shortened in the triplet/quad pregnancy.

What are My Recommendations?

I believe that all high order multiple pregnancies should have fFN tests done every two weeks (24, 26, 28, 31, 32 weeks). A positive test at any time should prompt very intensive management because delivery is usually not too far off. Hospitalization and cortic steroids are indicated. Tocolytic drugs (magnesium sulfate) and antibiotics, could also be started as many patients will rupture their membranes prior to delivery.

Some preliminary data we have obtained supports treating triplet or quadruplet pregnancies with steroids (prednisone or dexamethasone) if they have a positive fFN test. We have extended these pregnancies by more than a month compared to patients with positive fFN tests not receiving treatment doses of steroids. This is in addition to steroids for lung maturation.

We are still trying to determine which interventions will work (if any). This test is an exciting new advance, and as more experience is gained, physicians will be better able to provide care for these special pregnancies.

Will an Aspirin a Day
Keep the Doctor Away?

by John P. Elliott, M.D.

Multifetal pregnancies (triplets and quadruplets) are at risk for a number of complications. The most dangerous of these are the "3 P's: preterm labor, preterm rupture of membranes, and preeclampsia (toxemia). Much has been written about the first two P's, so we will discuss the third P – or preeclampsia.

What is preeclampsia? It is a disease that only occurs in pregnancy. There is no known reason why one woman gets it and others don't. It occurs in about 8% of singleton pregnancies and perhaps 20% of twins. Triplets may be at a 30-40% risk and in our quad pregnancies (13), preeclampsia occurred in 11 (85%). Women who are more likely to develop the disease include: first pregnancy (excluding miscarriages), extremes of age (younger or older), multiple gestation, chronic hypertension, renal disease, lupus, or diabetes.

Preeclampsia is caused by an imbalance in two chemicals in the body. Thromboxane is produced in platelets and when released in the blood stream causes the arteries in the body to constrict or become narrower. Prostacyclin is produced in the cells that line the walls of the arteries and it causes the arteries to dilate or widen. In women developing preeclampsia, the release of thromboxane dominates and the arteries narrow. In order to get the oxygen and nutrients to the organs of the body, the heart must pump harder (or increase the pressure generated) which leads to an increase in blood pressure.

Think of a garden hose that becomes kinked. To get the same amount of water out of the end of the hose, the pressure at the faucet (heart) must be increased. There is some kidney damage (not usually permanent) that causes protein to be lost in your urine (your doctor checks for that at each visit). The increased blood pressure plus loss of protein forces fluid out of your blood vessels into the surrounding tissue which leads to edema or swelling. This is preeclampsia.

Symptoms that you might experience are headache (usually severe), visual changes, sudden weight gain and swelling, and a heartburn-like pain below the breastbone or right rib cage. Higher-order multiple gestation will often develop a special kind of preeclampsia called HELLP syndrome. It is named for Hemolysis, Liver damage, and Low Platelets. Blood tests will diagnose this problem including: uric acid test, liver function test, and a platelet count. You don't have to have elevated blood pressure or protein in your urine to have HELLP syndrome.

Preeclampsia can cause seizures, stroke, kidney failure, and death, so it is a disease to be respected. The disease is cured by delivery and the mother will usually recover over a one-week period without long-term complications. All usually goes well if preeclampsia develops at term (36-42 weeks), but if it occurs earlier than that, then what is best for mom (delivery) may place the baby(ies) at risk for prematurity.

Can anything be done to prevent preeclampsia? Yes! There is scientific evidence that low-dose aspirin (81 mg), or baby aspirin, can affect preeclampsia. Those who take one low-dose aspirin a day have a lower incidence of preeclampsia, and if it does develop it appears later in pregnancy and is milder. This becomes very important in a higher-order multiple pregnancy where prematurity is almost a certain thing.

If we can minimize the need to deliver because of preeclampsia, then preterm labor and premature rupture of membranes become the main worries. Patients should not take an adult aspirin – only a baby aspirin. The baby aspirin selectively inhibits thromboxane without affecting prostacyclin, restoring the balance. A full adult aspirin (325 mg) inhibits both chemicals and can create problems in both mother and baby. One mother was so good about not taking aspirin that she was taking baby Tylenol for several weeks before we discovered the error. Baby Tylenol does not work for this problem.

The low dose aspirin should be started early in your pregnancy (we begin at 14-16 weeks) and taken one a day until delivery. **This should be done only in consultation with your physician.** A baby aspirin a day may indeed keep the doctor away.

The Erickson children, Faribault, Minnesota

Fatty Liver and HELLP Syndrome Followup

[Printed in Science Daily June 7, 1999]

Genetic Testing and Modified Diets May Save Babies Born With Genetic Defect

Winston-Salem, N.C. – Genetic testing and dietary modification may save the lives of children born with a defect in the gene controlling fatty acid breakdown, a Wake Forest University Baptist Medical Center physician reported in the June 3, 1999 issue of the New England Journal of Medicine.

Jamal A. Ibdah, M.D., Ph.D., assistant professor of internal medicine (gastroenterology), said screening women who develop a type of liver disease late in pregnancy – and their newborns – for the genetic defect could be lifesaving for the newborn.

Ibdah and his colleagues identified the genetic defect in 24 infants or toddlers who had come in with liver, heart or muscular abnormalities suggestive of defects in the body's use of fatty acids – which ordinarily are used to supply energy and for other essential functions. Eight of the infants died – seven almost immediately and the others died 18 months later, despite treatment.

"The remaining 16 patients are alive and are currently being treated with dietary modification," Ibdah said. "Eight of the surviving children are now older than 5 years and attending school."

The key to survival was a change in the diets of the affected children. "Dietary treatment in these and other fatty acid oxidation disorders dramatically reduces morbidity and mortality."

Ibdah said for infants with the genetic defect special formulas are available that both reduce the amount of fat and change the types of fat that the babies get. Older children must follow a special diet that accomplishes this same thing.

He said family histories showed previously unexplained sudden deaths in six siblings.

"The major finding in our study is that of the 24 others, 15 developed severe liver disease while carrying the babies," said Ibdah.

The research team speculates that the genetic defect in the fetus causes an accumulation of products of fatty acids produced by the fetus or the placenta that are particularly toxic to the liver of the mother. Further, they said, this effect may be exaggerated by the decreased ability of the mother to use fatty acids for energy during pregnancy.

He said the disease occurs in roughly one in every 14,000 pregnancies, and the mortality rate for the mother and babies ranges from 10 to 50 percent.

Some women develop a different, but apparently related disorder, which doctors call HELLP (Hemolysis, Elevated Liver enzymes and Low Platelets). HELLP is a more common maternal illness of late pregnancy, occurring in about one in every 200 pregnancies. Between 1 and 3 percent of the mothers die, while between 20 and 35 percent of the infants die in severe cases.

Of the 15 mothers with liver disease in the study, 11 had acute fatty liver, while four had HELLP.

Testing those mothers, their partners and the infants for the defect soon after birth could mean early diagnosis in the infant before problems can develop, essentially avoiding the complications. "We can save the babies by screening for this genetic defect" Ibdah said. "Screening can also help physicians better advise these mothers regarding the risk of future pregnancies."

The genetic test is available at the Wake Forest University Baptist Medical Center and at some other academic medical centers.

The study was supported by the National Institute of Diabetes and Digestive and Kidney Diseases and the American Digestive Health Foundation. The team also included investigators from the University of Texas Southwestern Medical Center in Dallas, the Mayo Clinic and the Washington University School of Medicine in St. Louis.

Scheduling Chart (The Triplet Connection)
In columns, state times and amounts

Name/date	Stool	Wet	Breast	Bottle	Water	Juice	Food	Vita	Rxs	Other	Temp	Weight	Bed	Bath	Cared for by

Suggested Resources

American Dietetic Association. (800) 366-1655 or (800) 877-1600.

Board Certification Line. If you want to know if your physician is board certified, call (800) 776-CERT (2378). Not all physicians may be listed, but the majority are.

Center for Loss in Multiple Birth (CLIMB). By and for parents who have experienced the death of one, both or all their children during a twin, triplet or higher-order multiple pregnancy, or in infancy or childhood. Also provides resources and support for those who are now pregnant and know that one or more of the babies have died in utero or are likely to lose an infant in utero or following birth. Has an active parent contact list available to network with others in similar situations. To receive the publication, **Our Newsletter**, contact Jean Kollantai, P.O. Box 91377, Palmer, AK 99645, (907) 222-5321, or Lisa Fleischer (907) 274-7029. E-mail climb@pobox.alaska.net ; website www.climb-support.org.

Center for Study of Multiple Birth. 33 E. Superior Street, Suite 464, Chicago, IL 60611 (312) 266-9093. E-mail lgk395@nwu.edu .

Childhelp U.S.A. An organization to help prevent child abuse with 24-hour telephone counseling. Free of charge. Anonymous. (800-4-A-CHILD).

Coalition for Positive Outcomes in Pregnancy (CPOP). A national partnership of organizations concerned about families and their pregnancy outcomes. 507 Capitol Court N.E. Suite 200, Washington, DC 20002. (202) 544-7499, Fax (209) 546-7105.

Family Advantage. A membership internet site providing professional advice on topics such as strengthening marriage, managing infants and toddlers, child help issues, school issues, improving financial status, depression and a thousand and one other issues. Call: toll-free 1 (800) 526-7793. E-mail alscores@itsnet.com. Website www.family advantage.net. Reduced membership for referrals through The Triplet Connection at $3.50 per month, 6 month minimum.

Group B Strep Association. Website www.groupbstrep.org (919) 932-5344.

6

LaLeche League International. 1400 N. Meacham Rd, P.O. Box 4079, Schaumburg, IL 60173-4048 (847) 519-7730 www.lalecheleague.org

Prevent Child Abuse America. A place to report child abuse or request resources for help. (800-CHILDREN). E-mail pca_wyo@msn.com

National Mothers of Twins Organization. P.O. Box 438, Thompson Station, TN 37179. (800) 243-2276. E-mail nomotc@aol.com web: www.nomotc.org.

Sidelines National Support Network. (For mothers on bedrest). P.O. Box 1808, Laguna Beach, CA 92652. Candace (949) 497-2265; Dannise (760) 598-5331; Diane (949) 581-5266; Tracy (719) 488-0266. E-mail sidelines@ sidelines.org; www.sidelines.org.

The Twins Foundation. An international non-profit organization established by twins to collect, preserve, and communicate information about twins and twin research. Quarterly newsletter. P.O. Box 6043, Providence, RI 02940-6043 (401) 729-1000.

Twin To Twin Transfusion Syndrome Foundation. Mary Slaman-Forsythe, Founder and President. Executive director Linda DeAngelis. 411 Longbeach Parkway, Bay Village, OH 44140. National Office (440) 899-TTTS. E-mail tttsfound@aol.com web www.tttsfoundation.org

Twinless Twins Support Group, Int'l. Group to offer support for parents and families who have lost one or more children who are twins or higher-order multiples. Dr. Raymond W. Brandt, Founder/Director. 11220 St. Joe Road, Fort Wayne, IN 46835. (219) 627-5414. E-mail twinless@iserve.net or twinworld1@aol.com web www.fwi.com/twinless

SHARE Pregnancy and Infant Loss Support, Inc. National SHARE office: St. Joseph Health Center, 300 First Capitol Drive, St. Charles, MO 63301 (800) 821-6819. E-mail share@nationalshareoffice.com web www.nhationalshareoffice.com

WIC (Women, Infants, Children). You may find details about the WIC program in your area by checking the white pages of the phone pages, looking under WIC, or call toll-free 1-(888)-WIC-WORKS.

Facts About Triplet Births

From <u>Trends and Outcomes from 1971-1994,</u>
A Summary of the Latest U.S. Government Report

- There were more triplets born in the first *half* of the 1990's than during the whole decade of the 1980's.
- The average birth weight of a triplet was 3 lbs., 12 oz.
- The average triplet gestational age at birth was 32 completed weeks with most triplets arriving between 34 and 36 weeks.
- From 1983-1991 mortality rates (death rates) of triplets dropped by 40%
- Triplets born at less than 28 weeks gestation had a higher mortality rate than comparable singletons. But triplets born from 28-36 weeks had comparable or better outcome than singletons of comparable gestation.
- Singletons did best born at or near term (37-40 weeks). Triplets did best when born between 34-36 weeks gestation.

Endnotes

Vital and Health Statistics from the Centers for Disease Control and Prevention/ National Center for Health Statistics. <u>Triplet Births: Trends and Outcomes, 1971- 94</u> (January 1997).

Related Reading and Viewing

Harrison, Helen. *The Premature Baby Book*. New York: St. Martin's Press, 1983.

Ilse, Sherokee. *A Shattered Dream*. Long Lake, MN: Wintrgreen Press, 1985. Wintergreen Press, 3630 Eileen Street, Maple Plain, MN 55359 (612) 765-1303.

Ilse, Sherokee. *Empty Arms: Coping with Miscarriage, Stillbirth and Infant Death*. Maple Plain, MN: Wintergreen Press, 3630 Eileen Street, Maple Plain, MN 55359 (612) 765-1303.

Katz, Michael, MD, Pamela Gill, RN, Judith Turiel, RN, *Preventing Preterm Birth: A Parent's Guide*. San Francisco: Health Publishing Co., 1988. (The paperback copy is $14.95, including shipping. Remit payment to C.P.M.C., Perinatal Education and Lactation Center, P. O. Box 7999, San Francisco, CA 94120.)

Luke B, Tamar Eberlein. *When You're Expecting Twins, Triplets or Quads*. Harper Perennial. 1999.

Rich, Laurie A. *When Pregnancy Isn't Perfect*, Larata Press, New York. 1996.

Triplets: Putting the Pieces Together. Video chronicling the experiences of a family who learns they are expecting triplets, their pregnancy experience, c-section delivery, newborn experience, and support group. Injoy Productions (800) 326-2082. Special price for home viewing $24.95 for Triplet Connection members (normally $99.95).

The Buettner children, Barrington, Illinois

6

Notes